Teaching with Everyday Manipulatives

Grades 4-6

Written by Melanie Komar
Illustrated by Amanda Smith and S&S Learning Materials

About the Author: Melanie Komar is an elementary public school teacher. She is the author of over 50 books for teachers and parents.

ISBN 978-1-55035-809-4
Copyright 2007
All Rights Reserved * Printed in Canada

Permission to Reproduce

Permission is granted to the individual teacher who purchases one copy of this book to reproduce the student activity material for use in his/her classroom only. Reproduction of these materials for an entire school or for a school system, or for other colleagues or for commercial sale is strictly prohibited. No part of this publication may be transmitted in any form or by any means, electronic, mechanical, recording or otherwise without the prior written permission of the publisher. "We acknowledge the financial support of the Government of Canada through the Book Publishing Industry Development Program (BPIDP) for this project."

Published in the United States by:
On The Mark Press
3909 Witmer Road PMB 175
Niagara Falls, New York
14305
www.onthemarkpress.com

Published in Canada by:
S&S Learning Materials
15 Dairy Avenue
Napanee, Ontario
K7R 1M4
www.sslearning.com

At A Glance

Learning Expectations	Pages 12–26	Pages 27–40	Pages 41–50	Pages 51–60	Pages 61–71
Numeration & Operations					
• Numeration and place value	•		•		
• Arithmetic functions with whole numbers, rational numbers, and integers (break down to add/subtract, multiply/divide, rationals, integers)	•		•	•	•
• Fractions, decimals, and percents	•		•	•	•
Measurement					
• Distance, in appropriate units		•	•		
• Time, in appropriate units			•	•	
• Perimeter and area			•		
• Volume and surface area			•		
Geometry					
• Two and three dimensional shapes	•	•	•		•
• Symmetry and translation		•			
Data & Probability					
• Chance and probability				•	
• Data collection and management				•	•
• Measurement of central tendency				•	
Algebra					
• Patterns and variables					•
• Graphical representation					•

Teaching Math with Everyday Manipulatives

Table of Contents

At a Glance 2

Teacher Rubric 4

Student Rubric 5

Teacher Suggestions 6

Number Sense and Numeration 6

Geometry 27

Measurement 40

Data and Probability 53

Algebra 65

Teaching Math with Everyday Manipulatives

Teacher Assessment Rubric

Student's Name: _____

Each project can be evaluated in many possible ways. The following rubric is just one way to evaluate these open-ended projects. It is based on a four-point scale.

- **4** The student demonstrates full understanding of all concepts. All work is complete and correct.
- **3** The student demonstrates a good understanding of the concepts. The student has few errors or misunderstandings.
- **2** The student demonstrates limited understanding. The student completes part of the activity incorrectly.
- **1** The student demonstrates little understanding or effort. The student does not complete the activity properly.

Level	4	3	2	1	N/A
Prepared for class					
Puts forth best effort					
Stays on task until completion					
Uses appropriate strategies to find solution; implements a plan to arrive at correct solution					
Explains mathematical thinking					
Demonstrates understanding of problem					
Labels work correctly and neatly					
Works cooperatively with others					
Makes connections to the real world					

Teaching Math with Everyday Manipulatives

Student Self-Assessment Rubric

Name: _____

Think about the learning in math that you have done. Assess yourself.

	Always or Almost Always ✔	Sometimes ✔	Need to Improve ✔
✔ I attend math lessons regularly.			
✔ I listen attentively.			
✔ I ask questions when I don't understand something.			
✔ I get along well with others.			
✔ I use materials properly.			
✔ My work is neat and complete.			
✔ I come to class prepared and ready to learn.			
✔ I tidy up after myself.			

Teaching Math with Everyday Manipulatives

Teacher Suggestions:

You should find many of these activities adaptable in terms of actual materials used. For example, if the activity suggests "buttons", often "pennies" can be used. Many activities suggest a game to play and implies that the games are 2 Player games, however, many activities can have more than two students and often, a single person can follow the steps alone. Finally, most of the activities are suitable for the average Grade 4, 5, or 6 student. While some activities will be quite challenging for Grade 4 or review for Grade 6, many can be adapted to each of the grade levels. Teachers can set the standard that they expect their students to achieve by showing examples of students who are performing the activity at the expected level. For example, save a student sample of a graph or pattern (take a picture if it was done with manipulatives) of a suitable level of work and leave it at the centre. Students working below or above grade level should be encouraged to work to the best of their own ability. Students who achieve below grade level results should be encouraged to watch and learn from others and observe how they are getting their results. Students working above grade level should be encouraged to model how they are working through the activity. Encourage peer teaching whenever possible.

Number Sense and Numeracy

Overview:

Number sense and numeration/operations is the ability to relate numbers to the quantities they represent. Numeration/operations are the computations that students perform with numbers. Manipulatives should be used to help students use representations, develop mathematical thinking and reasoning skills and to create problem solving strategies.

The NCTM Standards for the Junior Grade levels suggest that students should:

- understand the place-value structure of the base-ten number system and be able to represent and compare whole numbers and decimals;
- recognize equivalent representations for the same number and generate them by decomposing and composing numbers;
- develop understanding of fractions as parts of unit wholes, as parts of a collection, as locations on number lines, and as divisions of whole numbers;
- use models, benchmarks, and equivalent forms to judge the size of fractions;
- recognize and generate equivalent forms of commonly used fractions, decimals, and percents;

- explore numbers less than 0 by extending the number line and through familiar applications;
- describe classes of numbers according to characteristics such as the nature of their factors;
- understand various meanings of multiplication and division;
- understand the effects of multiplying and dividing whole numbers;
- identify and use relationships between operations, such as division as the inverse of multiplication, to solve problems;
- understand and use properties of operations, such as the distributivity of multiplication over addition;
- develop fluency with basic number combinations for multiplication and division and use these combinations to mentally compute related problems;
- develop fluency in adding, subtracting, multiplying, and dividing whole numbers;
- develop and use strategies to estimate the results of whole-number computations and to judge the reasonableness of such results;
- develop and use strategies to estimate computations involving fractions and decimals in situations relevant to students' experience;
- use visual models, benchmarks, and equivalent forms to add and subtract commonly used fractions and decimals;
- select appropriate methods and tools for computing with whole numbers from among mental computation, estimation, calculators, and paper and pencil according to the context and nature of the computation and use the selected method or tools.

The activities suggested in this book should, with regular practice over time, allow students to develop stronger number and numeration/operations skills.

Teacher Preparation Notes:

Spinning in Circles *(page 14)*
You will need to fill in the fractions that you would like converted to decimals, appropriate for your students' level. You can photocopy the blank sectioned circle many times and fill in one with fractions to be reduced or fractions to be converted to a decimal or decimals to be converted to fractions. Make several different versions so that the students can use different spinners each time. You may want to "code" them according to what level they are at for easy future reference. Grade 4 example: fraction to reduced fraction 3/6 4/12 5/25; fraction to decimal 1/10 66/100; decimal to fraction 0.2 0.65 0.08

Dice Fractions *(page 18)*
Using a wooden cube, write fractions on it that are appropriate for your class, (e.g., 1/2, 1/4, 1/3 for Grade 4; 1/6, 1/5, for Grade 5; 2/3, 3/5 for Grade 6)

Equality Pies *(page 19)*
Divide the paper plates (or circles) into 3rds or 5ths or 8ths, etc., depending on your students' skill level. You may even want to challenge them by not having the pies divided into equal sections, but instead combining, for example two 8ths, so that the pie has one 1/4 section and six 1/8 sections.

Dividing Dice *(page 21)*
Using 2 blank cubes and a permanent marker, create 2 die for this game using numbers appropriate for your students' skill level. For practice or review of simpler long division use small, even digit numerals for the divisor die (2, 2, 4, 4, 6, 8) and large, even digit numerals for the dividend die (e.g., 24, 36, 40, 48, 56, 80) which reduces the possibility of having a remainder. (Eliminate the possibility of having a remainder entirely by filling in the dividend die with only common multiples of the numerals on the divisor die.) For practice with more complicated long division, with remainders, use larger numerals on the divisor die, and large 3 or 4 digit numerals on the dividend die.

Estimating Decimals *(page 22)*
The students will be estimating multiplication. Make 2 sets of cards, in different colors. One set will be a whole number (put a multiplication sign in front of the whole number) and the other set will be a decimal. Choose numerals appropriate for your students' skill level.

Bull's Eye Estimates *(page 23)*
Use small paper plates, or cut out circles about the size of small paper plates. Draw about 3 circumference rings around the plate and one numeral in the middle to make it appear as a "bull's eye". Note: for easiest skill level use 3-digit "bull's eye" numerals that are multiples of 100 or of 10 (i.e., 400, 210, etc.). Then move on to multiples of 10 or 5 (i.e., 315 or 950). Increase the difficulty for your class, as required. For each "bull's eye" circle, have an index card that matches it (they should both be clearly lettered to indicate that they are a match).

Examples:

Target 210   Matching Card:

Column A	Column B
2	2
4	4
5	5
10	10
20	20
100	100

Target 315   Matching Card:

Column A	Column B
2	15
3	50
5	58
10	60
15	63
20	66
25	70
100	100

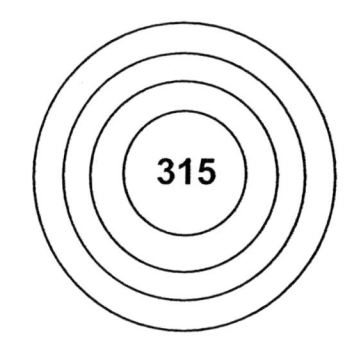

Teaching Math with Everyday Manipulatives

Name: _____

Estimation Jars

Number Sense and Numeracy

You Will Need:

- small objects (dried beans, pennies, buttons, etc.)
- clear containers

Steps:

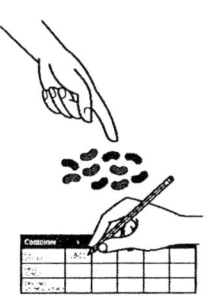

1. Fill a container with the objects.

2. Estimate how many you think are in the container. Record your guess in the chart below.

3. Next, count the objects. In the chart, record the actual number.

4. Fill the container with different objects and repeat steps 2 and 3.

5. Try using different containers to see which container holds more.

6. After several times of guessing and counting, find the **differences** between each guess and actual number.

Container	1	2	3	4	5
My Estimate					
Actual Number					
Difference (Estimate – Actual)					

Make It a Game!

1. You and another player can both try guessing how many objects are in the containers.

2. Find the differences between each guess and actual number, and **add** all the differences together to figure out who had the closest guess overall!

© On The Mark Press • S&S Learning Materials

OTM-1134 • SSK1-34 Teaching Math with Everyday Manipulatives

Teaching Math with Everyday Manipulatives

Name: _____

Place Value

You Will Need:

- index cards numbered 0 to 9

Steps:

1. Take any 5 numbers. Record the numbers that you chose.

   _____ _____ _____ _____ _____

2. Arrange them to make the smallest even-number 5-digit number possible.

Ten Thousands	Thousands	Hundreds	Tens	Ones
_____	_____	_____	_____	_____

3. Arrange them to make the largest even-number 5-digit number possible.

Ten Thousands	Thousands	Hundreds	Tens	Ones
_____	_____	_____	_____	_____

4. Arrange them to make the smallest odd-number 5-digit number possible.

Ten Thousands	Thousands	Hundreds	Tens	Ones
_____	_____	_____	_____	_____

5. Arrange them to make the largest odd-number 5-digit number possible.

Ten Thousands	Thousands	Hundreds	Tens	Ones
_____	_____	_____	_____	_____

Make It a Game!

1. Each player starts with their own set of numbered cards, face down.
2. Decide on a rule about what kind of number you are going to make (for example, "largest even-number").
3. At the same time, each player will choose any 5 cards from their pile and make the number that follows the rule.
4. The first person to correctly make the number scores a point.
5. The first player to score 5 points wins.

Tip: You can also play with more than 5 cards to make bigger numbers.

Number Sense and Numeracy

© On The Mark Press • S&S Learning Materials

Teaching Math with Everyday Manipulatives

Name: _____

Number Contest

Number Sense and Numeracy

You Will Need:

- 2 die each numbered 0, 1, 2, 3, 4, and 5
- 2 Players

Steps:

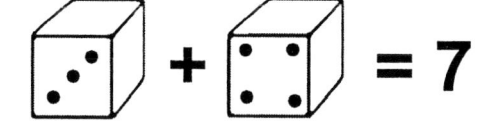

1. Player 1 rolls both die and adds the numbers.

2. In the Player 1 column, fill in any space on the first row with that number. If the total is 10, use a zero.

3. Player 2 rolls both die and fills in one space in their column on the first row.

4. Repeat until all spaces in the first row are filled in.

5. The player who creates the largest number is the winner and gets a point. Put a checkmark after your row if you created the largest number.

Tip: If you are just learning this game, use 5 spaces per line instead of 6.

Player 1: _____   Player 2: _____

1. __ __ __ __ __ __   __ __ __ __ __ __

2. __ __ __ __ __ __   __ __ __ __ __ __

3. __ __ __ __ __ __   __ __ __ __ __ __

4. __ __ __ __ __ __   __ __ __ __ __ __

5. __ __ __ __ __ __   __ __ __ __ __ __

Extension:

Put a decimal between the fourth and fifth spaces!

Teaching Math with Everyday Manipulatives

Name: _____

Multiplying Mania

You Will Need:

- about 100 small objects (beans, buttons, pennies, etc.)

Steps:

1. Arrange the objects into groups of equal sets (for example, 3 sets of 4 beans).

2. a) Sketch a picture of the sets.
   b) Make 2 multiplication and 2 division sentences.

   Example: 3x4=12   4x3=12   12 ÷ 3=4   12 ÷ 4=3

3. Repeat steps 1 and 2.

Sketch:

Multiplication Sentences _____ = _____   _____ = _____

Division Sentences _____ = _____   _____ = _____

Sketch:

Multiplication Sentences _____ = _____   _____ = _____

Division Sentences _____ = _____   _____ = _____

Extension:

Instead of arranging the objects into sets, you can arrange them into an array.

Teaching Math with Everyday Manipulatives

Name: _____

Figuring Fractions

You Will Need:

- small objects about the size of a square on the grid (buttons, dried beans, etc.)

Steps:

1. On the grid, cover some of the squares with small objects.

2. Write a fraction for the amount of the grid that is covered. Reduce the fraction to lowest terms.

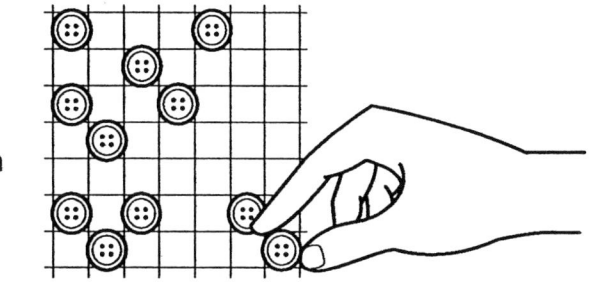

3. Repeat these steps 5 more times.

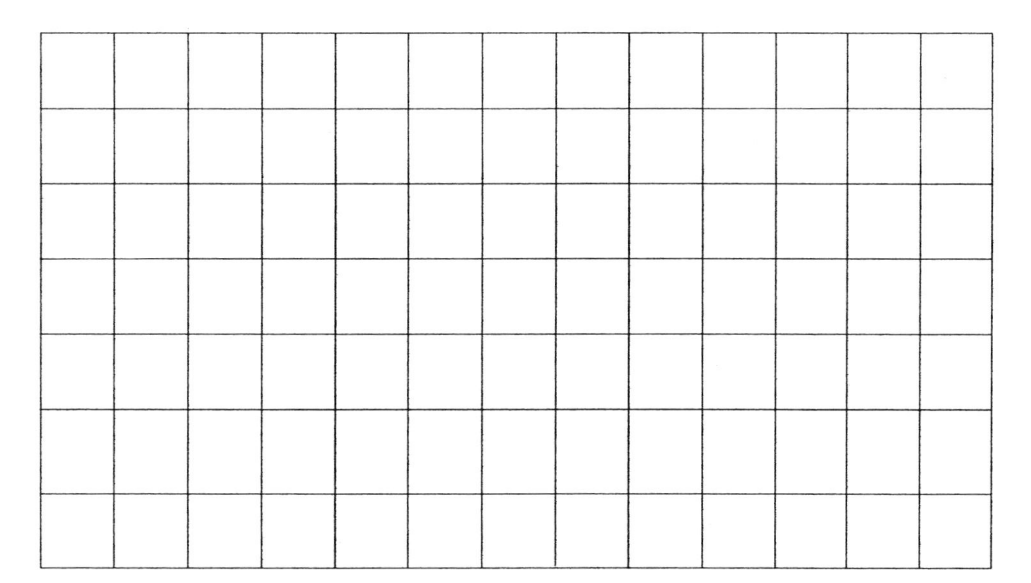

Fraction 1: _____ = _____   Fraction 2: _____ = _____   Fraction 3: _____ = _____

Fraction 4: _____ = _____   Fraction 5: _____ = _____   Fraction 6: _____ = _____

Extension:

When you get really good at making a fraction, try also writing a decimal for the amount of the grid covered. Then, try changing the fraction or the decimal into a percent to describe the amount covered.

Number Sense and Numeracy

© On The Mark Press • S&S Learning Materials

Teaching Math with Everyday Manipulatives

Name: _____

Spinning in Circles!

You Will Need:

- paperclip
- circle with fractions (see instructions page 7)

Steps:

1. Place the end of the paperclip in the center of circle. Hold the tip of your pencil in place and spin the paperclip.

2. Look at the pie piece on which the paperclip stops. Write the equivalent decimal for this fraction in the player 1 row below.

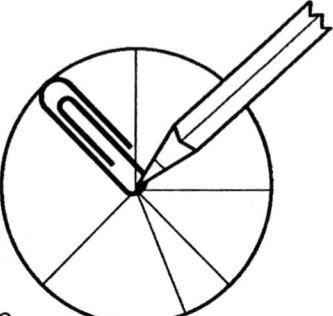

3. If you are playing with a partner, then player 2 takes their turn, repeating steps 1 and 2.

4. Keep playing until you fill in each space.

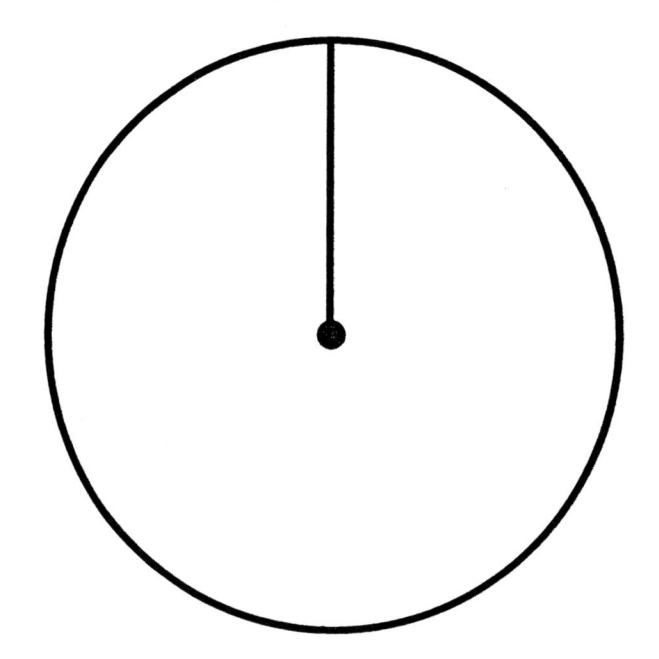

Player 1: _____ _____ _____ _____ _____ _____ _____ _____

Player 2: _____ _____ _____ _____ _____ _____ _____ _____

Teaching Math with Everyday Manipulatives

Name: _____

Multiple Arrays

You Will Need:

- grid paper (page 77)
- small objects (beans, counters, pennies, etc.)

Steps:

1. Cover part of the grid with small objects in an array.
2. Then, write a multiplication sentence for the array in the space below.
3. Repeat steps 1 and 2.

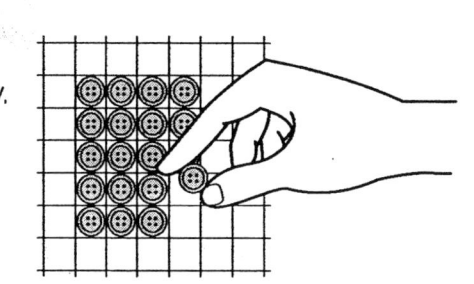

Array 1	Array 2	Array 3
____ = ____	____ = ____	____ = ____
Array 4	Array 5	Array 6
____ = ____	____ = ____	____ = ____
Array 7	Array 8	Array 9
____ = ____	____ = ____	____ = ____
Array 10	Array 11	Array 12
____ = ____	____ = ____	____ = ____

Make It a Game!

1. Find a partner, and have Player 1 cover part of the grid with objects in an array.
2. Player 2 writes the multiplication sentence for the array.
3. Player 1 checks the multiplication sentence and, if correct, gives Player 2 one point.
4. Switch roles.

Tip: Players can also make a multiplication sentence and ask the other Player to arrange the objects in that array.

Number Sense and Numeracy

Grid Division

You Will Need:

- grid paper (page 77)
- scissors
- glue

Steps:

1. Trace 4 rectangular shapes on the grid paper. Use straight lines along grid lines only. There may be some extra squares extending past one row or one column.

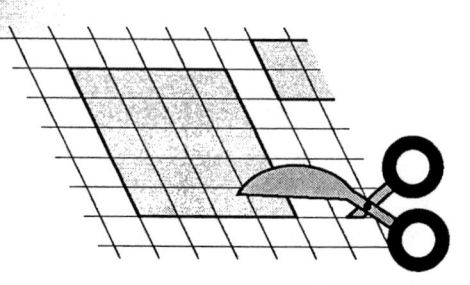

2. Cut out the shapes.

3. Glue each shape in a space below, and write a division question for each shape.

_____ = _____	_____ = _____
_____ = _____	_____ = _____

Make It a Game!

1. Find a partner, and both Players trace and cut out 4 rectangular shapes.
2. Trade shapes.
3. Glue each shape to your paper and write a division question for each shape.
4. Each Player gets a point for a correct division question. The first player to reach 5 points wins. (If there is a tie, you both win!)

Grid Fractions

You Will Need:

- grid paper (page 77)
- scissors
- glue

Steps:

1. Draw a rectangular on grid paper and cut it out.
2. In the rectangle, draw 3 straight lines. These lines should either be straight along the grid lines or dividing the rectangle into equal halves (triangles). You should now have 4 small shapes within your rectangle.
3. Label each shape inside the rectangle A, B, C, or D.
4. Glue the rectangle grid into the space below.
5. Write the fractions that each grid area represents.

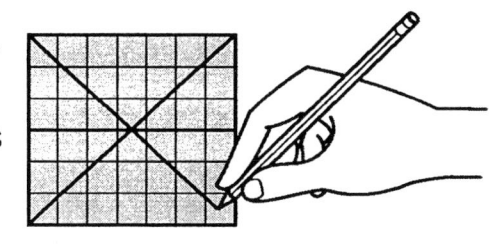

a) _____   b) _____   c) _____   d) _____

Make It a Game!

1. Find a partner, and both Players square off and cut out a rectangular section of the grid paper. Draw 3 straight lines along the grid lines in your rectangle.
2. Exchange grids and glue the grid (from the other Player) onto your own paper.
3. Glue each shape to your paper and write a division question for each shape.
4. Write the fractions that each grid area represents.

Dice Fractions

You Will Need:

- 20 to 40 small objects (pennies, beans, etc.) per Player
- Fraction Dice (see instructions page 7)

Steps:

1. Each Player takes the same amount of objects.
2. Player 1 rolls the dice and takes the exact fraction of the other Player's objects. If they cannot take the exact fraction rolled, they do not take anything. (Example: if Player 2 has 30 objects and Player 1 rolls 2/3, Player 2 takes 20 out of the 30 objects; if Player 2 rolls ¼, then he or she does not take any.)
3. Record your roll and actions in the Game Card below.
4. Players reverse their roles after each roll of the dice.
5. When one Player has taken away all the objects from the other Player, that Player wins.

Game Card

Roll	Fraction on dice	Number of objects my opponent has	Number of objects I take away
1			
2			
3			
4			
5			
6			
7			
8			
9			
10			

Teaching Math with Everyday Manipulatives

Name: _____

Equality Pies

You Will Need:

- paper plates (or cut-out circles) divided into equal sections (see instructions page 7)
- 2 sets of small objects (pennies, beans, buttons, etc.)

Steps:

1. Place object 1 in some of the sections, and object 2 in each of the other sections.

2. Draw a sketch of your "pie" and then record the ratio of one object to the second object (example: 1:3).

3. Repeat steps 1 and 2 with different objects.

Sketch	Ratio _____	Sketch	Ratio _____
Sketch	Ratio _____	Sketch	Ratio _____
Sketch	Ratio _____	Sketch	Ratio _____
Sketch	Ratio _____	Sketch	Ratio _____

Extension:

Write fractions that represent each object (for example, 1/4 and 3/4).

Lining Up Decimals

Steps:

1. Place a mark anywhere on the first number line below.

2. Record the decimal represented by the mark.

Example: 2.9   0 -!-!-!-!-!-!-!-!-!-!- 1 -!-!-!-!-!-!-!-!-!-!- 2 -!-!-!-!-!-!-!-!-✏-!- 3

3. On the second number line, put a mark on a different place and record the decimal.

4. Repeat these steps for all the number lines.

                                                                                                                    Decimal

1. 0--!--!--!--!--!--!--!--!--!--1--!--!--!--!--!--!--!--!--!--!--2-!--!--!--!--!--!--!--!--!--!--3   _____

2. 0--!--!--!--!--!--!--!--!--!--1--!--!--!--!--!--!--!--!--!--!--2-!--!--!--!--!--!--!--!--!--!--3   _____

3. 0--!--!--!--!--!--!--!--!--!--1--!--!--!--!--!--!--!--!--!--!--2-!--!--!--!--!--!--!--!--!--!--3   _____

4. 0--!--!--!--!--!--!--!--!--!--1--!--!--!--!--!--!--!--!--!--!--2-!--!--!--!--!--!--!--!--!--!--3   _____

5. 0--!--!--!--!--!--!--!--!--!--1--!--!--!--!--!--!--!--!--!--!--2-!--!--!--!--!--!--!--!--!--!--3   _____

6. 0--!--!--!--!--!--!--!--!--!--1--!--!--!--!--!--!--!--!--!--!--2-!--!--!--!--!--!--!--!--!--!--3   _____

7. 0--!--!--!--!--!--!--!--!--!--1--!--!--!--!--!--!--!--!--!--!--2-!--!--!--!--!--!--!--!--!--!--3   _____

8. 0--!--!--!--!--!--!--!--!--!--1--!--!--!--!--!--!--!--!--!--!--2-!--!--!--!--!--!--!--!--!--!--3   _____

9. 0--!--!--!--!--!--!--!--!--!--1--!--!--!--!--!--!--!--!--!--!--2-!--!--!--!--!--!--!--!--!--!--3   _____

10. 0--!--!--!--!--!--!--!--!--!--1--!--!--!--!--!--!--!--!--!--!--2-!--!--!--!--!--!--!--!--!--!--3   _____

Extension:

Record the fraction as well; reduced to lowest terms (for example, 2.9 is 2 9/10)

Dividing Dice

You Will Need:

- 2 dividing dice (see instructions page 8)

Steps:

1. Roll both die.
2. Record the 2 numbers you rolled.
3. Make a division question. Solve.
4. Repeat steps 1 to 3.

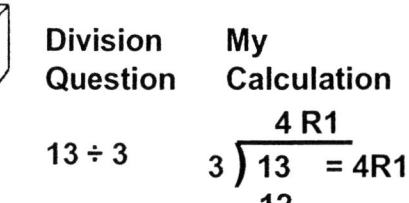

3   1

Division Question: $13 \div 3$

My Calculation:
$$3 \overline{)13} = 4R1$$
$$-12$$
$$1$$

	Dice 1	Dice 2	Division Question	My Calculation
1.			___ − ___	
2.			___ − ___	
3.			___ − ___	
4.			___ − ___	
5.			___ − ___	

Make It a Game!

1. Play in pairs and take turns rolling and solving. Check each other's answers.
2. Each time you solve the question correctly, you earn a point.
3. First Player to 10 wins.

Estimating Decimals

You Will Need:

- 2 sets of cards (see instructions page 8)

Steps:

1. Choose one card from each pile.
2. Place both cards on the table, one above the other, with the card with the multiplication sign under the other.
3. Estimate the product of the 2 numbers and record your answer.
4. Write down the question and figure out the actual answer.
5. Find the difference between the 2 products to find out how close your estimate was.
6. Repeat steps 1 to 5.

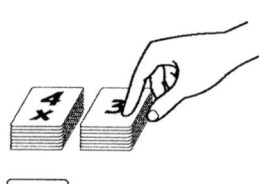

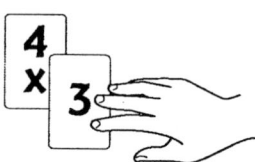

	Estimate	Calculation	Difference (Estimate – Actual Answer)
1.			
2.			
3.			
4.			
5.			

Make It a Game!

1. Player 1 chooses a card from one pile, and Player 2 chooses a card from the other pile.
2. Follow steps 2 to 4 above, doing your estimation and calculation silently.
3. Find the difference between the 2 products and that is your score.
4. Do this a total of 5 times. Add all your scores together and the player with the lowest overall score is the winner.

Name: _____

Bull's Eye Estimates!

You Will Need:

- Bull's Eye Targets (see instructions page 8)
- color-coded matching cards
- calculator

Steps:

1. Player 1 chooses a Bull's Eye Target and matching card.

2. Both Players individually choose one number from each column, the product of which they estimate will be closest to the bull's eye number.

3. Players use the calculator to find out who was closest to the bull's eye. That Player gets a point.

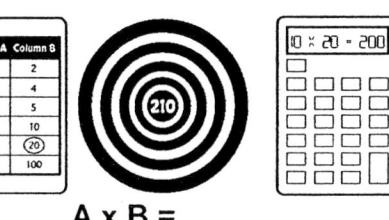

4. Next, Player 2 chooses a Bull's Eye Target and Matching Card and the game is repeated.

5. The Player with the most points at the end wins the game.

A x B = _____

Bull's Eye Target Number	Multiplication Question	Answer	Difference (Target – Answer)	Points
	___ x ___		___ – ___ = ___	
	___ x ___		___ – ___ = ___	
	___ x ___		___ – ___ = ___	
	___ x ___		___ – ___ = ___	
	___ x ___		___ – ___ = ___	

Teaching Math with Everyday Manipulatives

Name: _____

Array Division

You Will Need:

- array
- about 150 small objects (pennies, buttons, paper squares)

Steps:

1. Arrange the objects in an array. There may be objects that don't exactly fit into a row.

2. Sketch the array.

3. Write down a division number sentence that tells about the array, and solve.

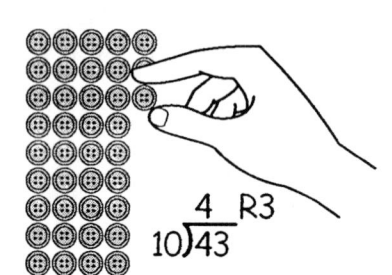

$10\overline{)43}$ = 4 R3

Sketch	Division Sentence	Calculation
	_____ ÷ _____	
	_____ ÷ _____	
	_____ ÷ _____	
	_____ ÷ _____	

Teaching Math with Everyday Manipulatives

Name: _____

Base Ten Estimation

You Will Need:

- base ten blocks (several each of ones, tens, hundreds, thousands) *(page 76)*

Steps:

1. Player 1 takes a random amount of ones, tens, hundreds, and thousands blocks and places them in front of Player 2.

2. Player 2 quickly estimates the number represented by the blocks in front of them. Record the estimate.

3. Count them to find the actual numbers. (**Hint:** Put all the thousands blocks together, then the hundreds, tens and ones.)

4. Record the actual number in digits and then in words.

5. Find the difference between the estimate and the actual answer.

6. Switch roles.

7. The Player with the lowest total differences at the end, wins.

Estimated Total	Actual Total	Difference (Estimated – Actual)
Total Differences:		

Teaching Math with Everyday Manipulatives

Name: _____

Adding Fractions with Cuisenaire Rods

Number Sense and Numeracy

You Will Need:

- Cuisenaire Rods (to create your own rods, do Cool Cuisenaire Rods page 54)

Steps:

1. Choose any 2 Cuisenaire Rods and record both fractions.

   1/7   7/1

2. Make an addition sentence with them, and solve.   1/7 + 7/1 = 7 1/7

Fraction 1	Fraction 2	Addition Sentence
		+ =
		+ =
		+ =
		+ =
		+ =
		+ =
		+ =

Make it a Game!

1. Player 1 chooses any 2 cuisenaire rods and gives them to Player 2.
2. Player 2 records the 2 fractions given to them and adds them.
3. Player 1 checks their work and, if correct, gives Player 2 one point.
4. Switch roles.
5. The player with the most points at the end wins.

© On The Mark Press • S&S Learning Materials

OTM-1134 • SSK1-34 Teaching Math with Everyday Manipulatives

Teaching Math with Everyday Manipulatives

Geometry

Overview:

Geometry is the study of spatial patterns and learning to make sense of objects and locations in their physical environment. Manipulatives should be used to help students focus on representations, reasoning skills and to develop mathematical arguments. The activities suggested in this book should, with regular practice over time, allow students to develop stronger geometry skills.

The NCTM Standards for the Junior Grade levels suggest that students should:

- identify, compare, and analyze attributes of two- and three-dimensional shapes and develop vocabulary to describe the attributes;
- classify two- and three-dimensional shapes according to their properties and develop definitions of classes of shapes such as triangles and pyramids;
- investigate, describe, and reason about the results of subdividing, combining, and transforming shapes;
- explore congruence and similarity;
- make and test conjectures about geometric properties and relationships and develop logical arguments to justify conclusions;
- describe location and movement using common language and geometric vocabulary;
- make and use coordinate systems to specify locations and to describe paths;
- find the distance between points along horizontal and vertical lines of a coordinate system;
- predict and describe the results of sliding, flipping, and turning two-dimensional shapes;
- describe a motion or a series of motions that will show that two shapes are congruent;
- identify and describe line and rotational symmetry in two- and three-dimensional shapes and designs;
- build and draw geometric objects;
- create and describe mental images of objects, patterns, and paths;
- identify and build a three-dimensional object from two-dimensional representations of that object;
- identify and draw a two-dimensional representation of a three-dimensional object;
- use geometric models to solve problems in other areas of mathematics, such as number and measurement;
- recognize geometric ideas and relationships and apply them to other disciplines and to problems that arise in the classroom or in everyday life.

Geometry

Teacher Preparation Notes:

All About Solids (page 34)

For this activity you need 2 shape cubes. One with a different drawing on each face: rectangular prism, hexagonal prism, triangular prism, square-based pyramid, triangular prism, pentagonal pyramid and the other with the words: name, faces, edges, perpendicular edges, parallel faces, and parallel edges written on each face.

Battleship (page 37)

In advance, laminate 2 copies of the coordinate grid (from page 37). Make 2 sets of "battleships" from sturdy strips of paper that will cover the squares of the grid in the following sizes 1, 2-square, 2, 3-square, 1, 4-square. Store these in labeled zip-lock bags or envelopes.

Congruent Angles (page 38)

Gather items with various assorted angles and put them together in a basket or container. Since the students will be required to measure the angles, choose items that have angles that are appropriate for your students' skill level. If you keep this activity out over an extended time, simply exchange the items frequently to keep it fresh. As they improve in their speed and accuracy, you may choose to include a timer or stopwatch to further challenge them.

Classifying 3D Shapes (page 39)

Either have the 3D shapes template available at this center, or you can do a prior lesson where all the students make their own 3D shapes.

Teaching Math with Everyday Manipulatives

Name: _____

Three Terrific Triangles

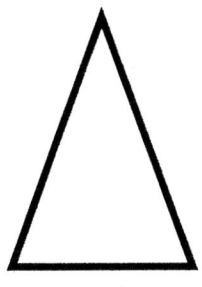

isosceles
(2 equal sides)

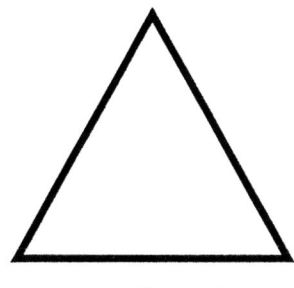

equilateral
(3 equal sides)

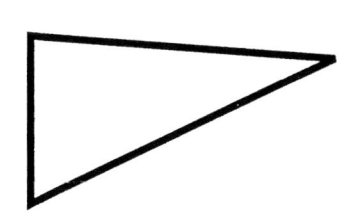

scalene
(no equal sides)

You Will Need:

- assorted lengths of popsicle sticks (or toothpicks or string or paper strips)
- ruler

Steps:

1. Make each of the three kinds of triangles.

2. Measure the sticks to find the ones with the lengths that you need.

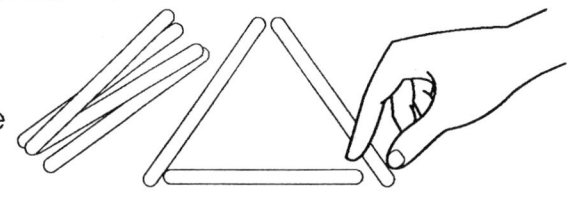

3. On your paper, arrange the sticks to make each kind of triangle.

4. Use your pencil to mark the corners of each of the triangles.

5. Remove the sticks.

6. Use your ruler to draw the outline of the triangles, using the corner marks that you made.

7. Label your triangles.

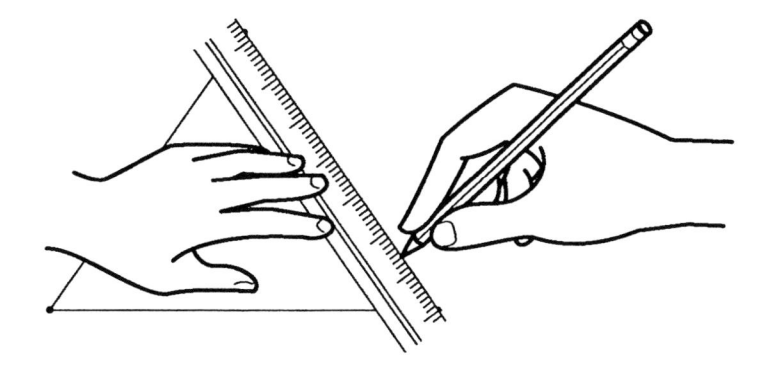

Name: _____

Triangle Classification

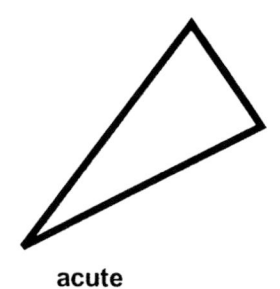

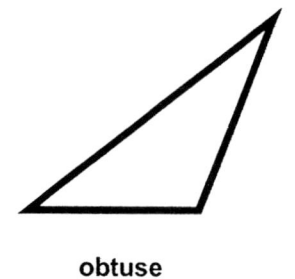

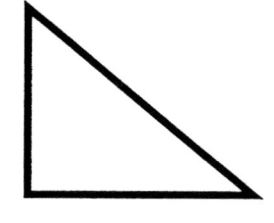

acute   obtuse   right-angle

You Will Need:

- toothpicks

Steps:

1. Create 6 different triangles. (**Tip:** Use 2, 3 or more toothpicks lined up together to create sides of different lengths.)

2. Complete the chart below for each triangle that you made.

Triangle Sketch	Kind of Triangle	Number of Acute Angles	Number of Obtuse Angles	Number of Right Angles
1.				
2.				
3.				
4.				
5.				
6.				

Shapes Are Everywhere!

You Will Need:

- old magazines, catalogs, flyers
- scissors and glue

Steps:

1. Look through the magazine to find the following shapes:

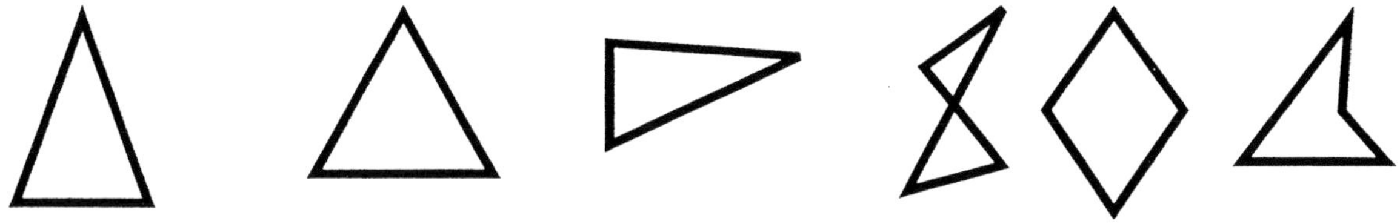

   isosceles triangle   equilateral triangle   scalene   quadrilaterals

2. Cut them out and glue them in the space below. Label them.

Teaching Math with Everyday Manipulatives   Name: _____

Spin the Line!

You Will Need:

- paperclip

Steps:

1. Put the paper clip in the middle of the circle (below) and hold it to the paper with your pencil.
2. Take turns spinning the paper clip around the pencil.
3. On the chart, draw an example of lines that the paper clip lands on.
4. The first person to fill in their side of the chart is the winner.

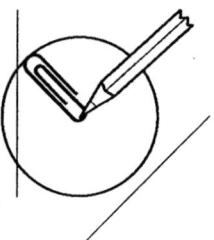

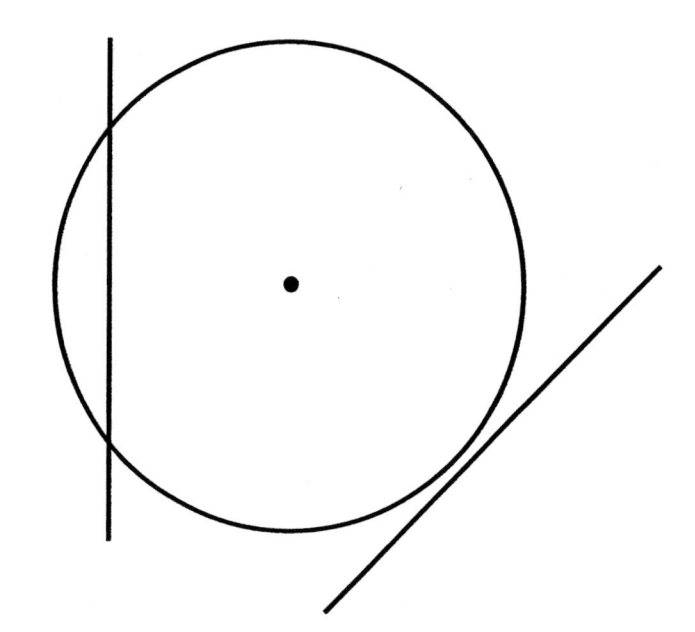

	Player 1: _____	Player 2: _____
Horizontal		
Vertical		
Parallel		
Intersecting		
Perpendicular		

Secret Polygon

You Will Need:

- ruler
- coloring pencil

Steps:

1. Using a ruler and pencil, each Player draws 6 different polygons.
2. Player 1 secretly thinks about one of the polygons on their paper.
3. Player 2 asks questions about the secret polygon.
   (**Example:** How many sides does it have? How many right angles does it have?)
   Each question asked is worth 1 point for the Player who chose the secret polygon.
4. When Player 2 thinks they know the secret polygon, point it out. Each incorrect guess gives the other Player two points, so be quite sure about your guess!
5. Players switch roles. The Player with the most points after three guesses per Player is the winner!

My Polygons

Score Card	Total
Points for Questions Asked *(1 point each)*	
Points for Incorrect Guesses *(2 points each)*	
Total Score	
Points for Questions Asked *(1 point each)*	
Points for Incorrect Guesses *(2 points each)*	
Total Score	
Points for Questions Asked *(1 point each)*	
Points for Incorrect Guesses *(2 points each)*	
Total Score	

Teaching Math with Everyday Manipulatives

Name: _____

All About Solids

You Will Need:

- 2 shape cubes (see instructions page 28)

Steps:

1. Player 1 rolls both dice.
2. On the chart, Player 1 fills in the answer of the second dice, about the solid rolled on the first dice. (If you roll a combination that you have already filled in, you miss your turn.)
3. Player 2 rolls both dice and fills in his or her chart.
4. Repeat steps 1 to 3. The first person to correctly fill in everything about all shapes is the winner.

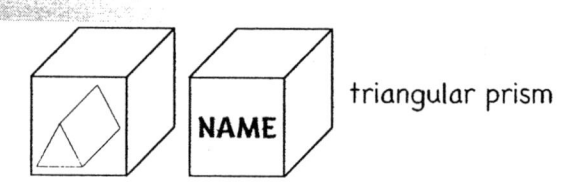

triangular prism

Type of Solid					
Name					
Number of Faces					
Number of Edges					
Number of Perpendicular Edges					
Number of Parallel Faces					
Number of Parallel Edges					

Teaching Math with Everyday Manipulatives

Name: _____

Design a Cube

You Will Need:

- scissors
- tape

Steps:

1. Use the template to make a hexomino (6 joined squares) that will fold into a cube.

2. Cut it out and fold it into a cube.

3. Now, design your own hexomino that is different from the one you just made. If it does not work, try another design.

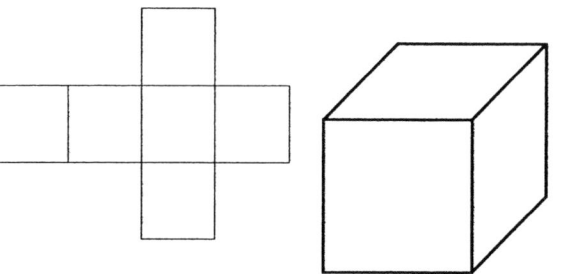

4. How many different hexominos can you fold into cubes? _____

Hexomino Template

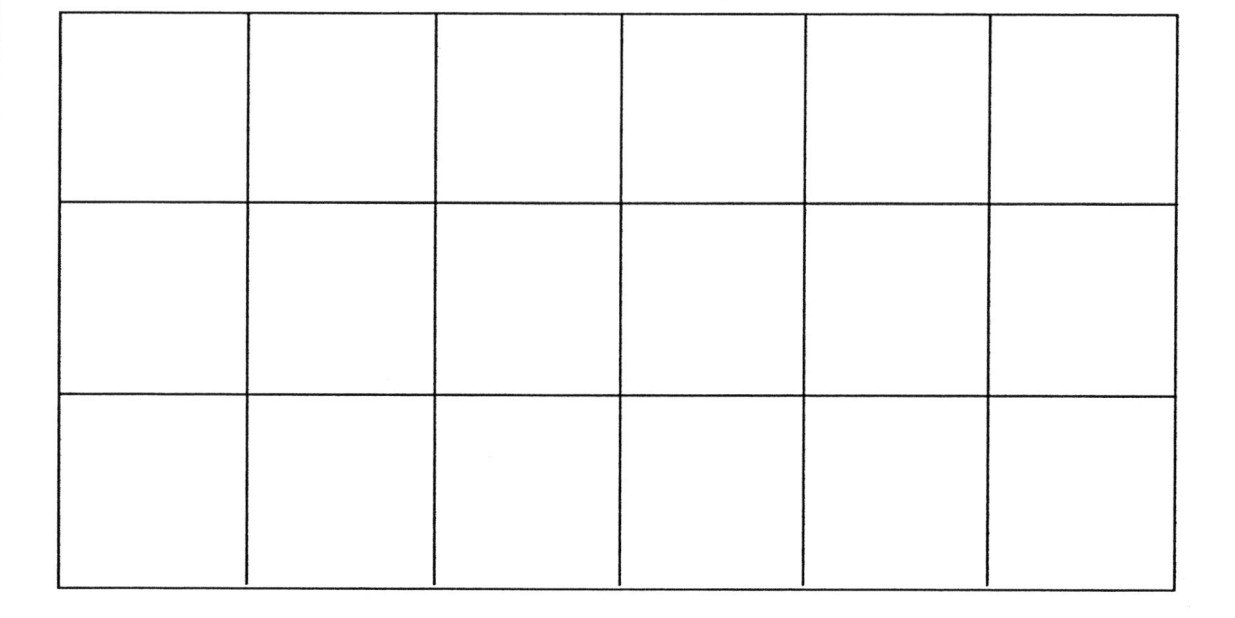

Extension:

Fold pentominos (5 joined squares) into a topless box.

Grid Lock

You Will Need:

- 5 each of two different small objects (**Example:** 5 beans and 5 pennies, or 5 red buttons and 5 yellow buttons)

Steps:

1. Place 10 objects on the coordinate grid provided below.

2. Write down the coordinates of each of the 10 objects.

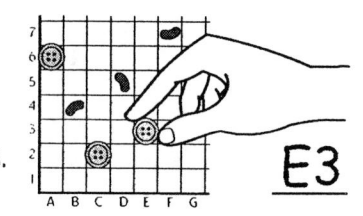

E3

Coordinate Grid

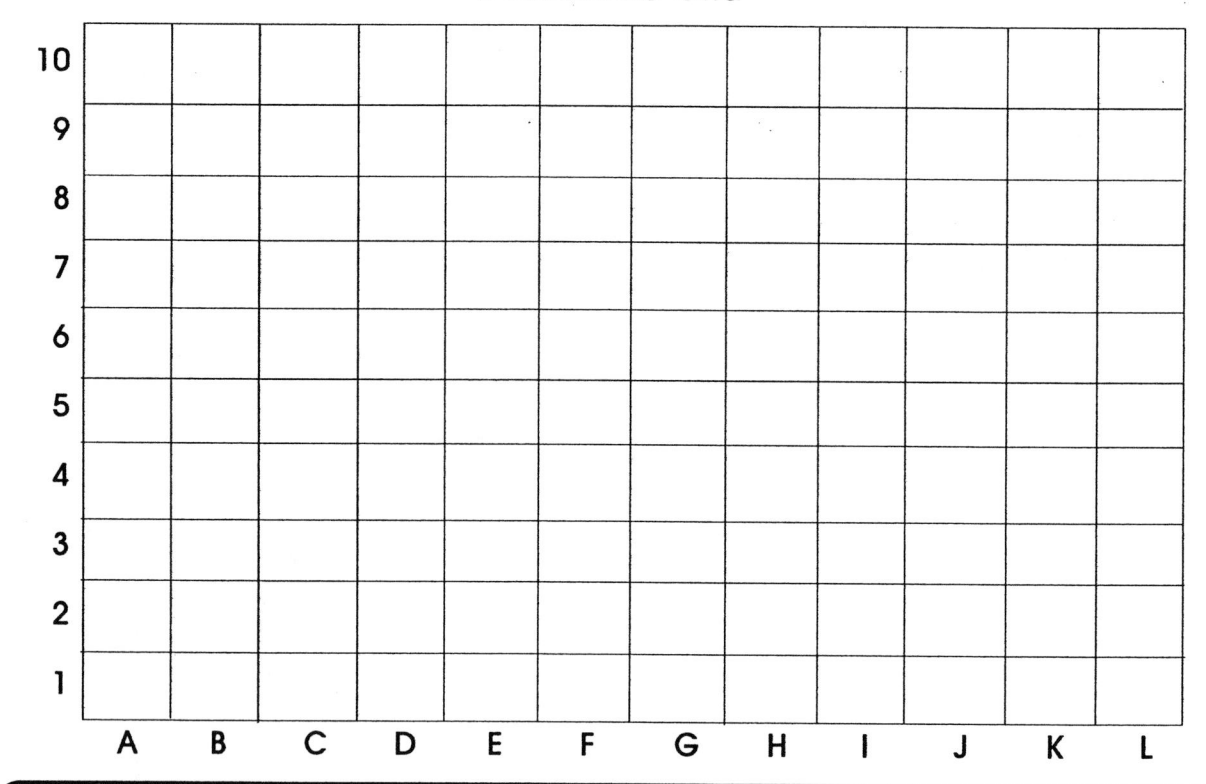

My Coordinates

1. _____   2. _____   3. _____   4. _____

5. _____   6. _____   7. _____   8. _____

9. _____   10. _____

Teaching Math with Everyday Manipulatives

Name: _____

Battleship

You Will Need:

- copy of the coordinate grid below for each player
- 2 sets of "battleships" (see instructions page 28)

Steps:

1. Each Player secretly places their "ships" on their own grid.
2. Take turns guessing a coordinate where you think the other player may have hidden a ship.
3. Keep track by putting a check mark on your grid when you guess correctly and an X if there is nothing there.
4. The first player to find all 4 of the other Players ships wins.

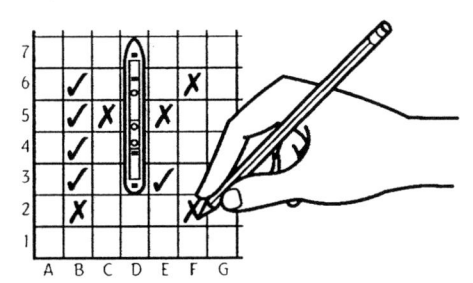

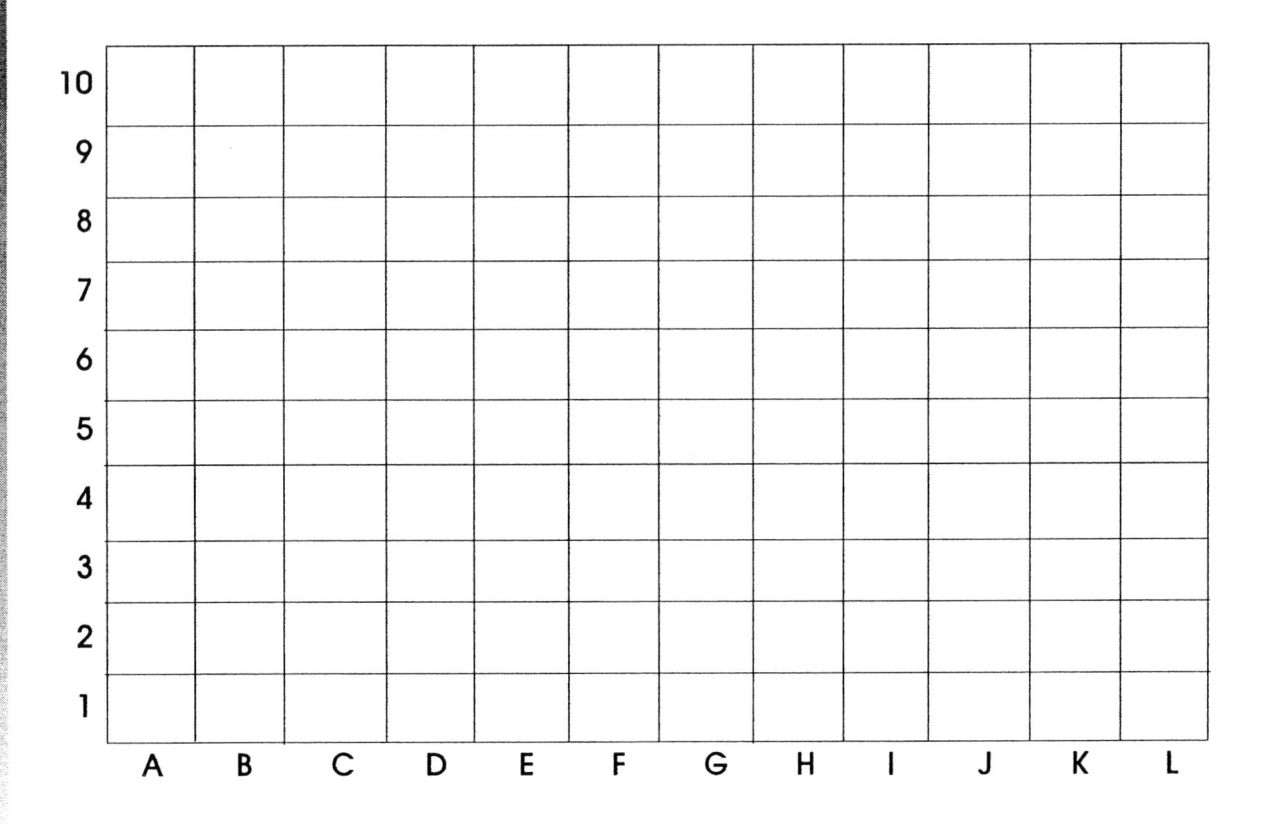

Coordinate Grid

Teaching Math with Everyday Manipulatives

Name: _____

Congruent Angles

You Will Need:

- items with different angles
- protractor

Steps:

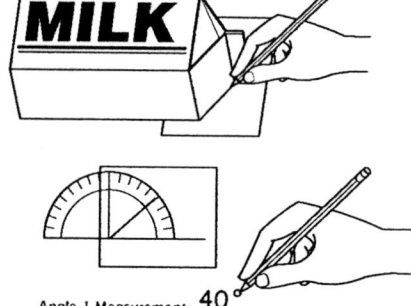

1. Choose an item and trace one angle on a sheet of paper.
2. Measure the angle with a protractor and record the measurement below.
3. Find another object with a congruent (same) angle and trace the angle.
4. Measure and record the second angle below.
5. Repeat steps 1 to 5 until you have traced 6 sets of congruent angles. Make sure that you do not trace the same angle that you have done before. For example, if your first angle is 90°, then you cannot choose another an angle with 90°.
6. How quickly did you trace 6 sets of congruent angles? _____

Angle 1 Measurement: 40

---

1. Angle 1 measurement: _____   Angle 2 measurement: _____
   Are these angles congruent? _____

2. Angle 1 measurement: _____   Angle 2 measurement: _____
   Are these angles congruent? _____

3. Angle 1 measurement: _____   Angle 2 measurement: _____
   Are these angles congruent? _____

4. Angle 1 measurement: _____   Angle 2 measurement: _____
   Are these angles congruent? _____

5. Angle 1 measurement: _____   Angle 2 measurement: _____
   Are these angles congruent? _____

6. Angle 1 measurement: _____   Angle 2 measurement: _____
   Are these angles congruent? _____

Teaching Math with Everyday Manipulatives

Name: _____

Classifying 3D Shapes

You Will Need:

- assorted small 3D objects
- Venn diagram (page 80)

Steps:

1. Think of a secret sorting rule and then sort the 3D shapes into the Venn diagram. (**Note:** some shapes may not fit the rule and can be left out.)
2. Sketch the objects below as you have sorted them. Write the sorting rule next to your sketch.
3. Repeat these steps using a new sorting rule until you have sketched and recorded 4 different sorting rules.
4. Recreate your sorting sketches for a friend, and see if he or she can guess each rule. You will need to cover the written rules with a piece of paper.

Sketch	Sketch
Rule: _____	Rule: _____
Sketch	Sketch
Rule: _____	Rule: _____

Teaching Math with Everyday Manipulatives

Measurement

Overview:

Measurement is assigning a numerical value to a given attribute by physically measuring it. It combines geometry and number strands. Manipulatives should be used to help students focus on choosing a unit of measure and comparing it to the object and reporting the measurement. Developing estimation strategies and understanding the relationship between various measurements are also a benefit of using manipulatives. The activities suggested in this book should, with regular practice over time, allow students to develop stronger measurement skills.

The NCTM Standards for the Junior Grade levels suggest that students should:

- understand such attributes as length, area, weight, volume, and size of angle and select the appropriate type of unit for measuring each attribute;
- understand the need for measuring with standard units and become familiar with standard units in the customary and metric systems;
- carry out simple unit conversions, such as from centimeters to meters, within a system of measurement;
- understand that measurements are approximations and how differences in units affect precision;
- explore what happens to measurements of a two-dimensional shape such as its perimeter and area when the shape is changed in some way;
- develop strategies for estimating the perimeters, areas, and volumes of irregular shapes;
- select and apply appropriate standard units and tools to measure length, area, volume, weight, time, temperature, and the size of angles;
- select and use benchmarks to estimate measurements;
- develop, understand, and use formulas to find the area of rectangles and related triangles and parallelograms;
- develop strategies to determine the surface areas and volumes of rectangular solids.

Teacher Preparation Notes:

Presenting Perimeters (page 42)

Put out items appropriate for your students to measure the perimeter. The items can be flat objects (book, envelope, CD case, etc.) or shapes cut out from sturdy paper.

If you have items with curves, you can show the students how to measure the perimeter with a piece of string.

Measurement

Area (page 45)

If you don't want a permanent record of the students work, you can laminate grid paper for this!

Shopping Time (page 46)

Gather themed related items such as small toys (toy store), plastic food (grocery store), books (book store), empty DVD/CD cases (movie/music store), school supplies, etc. If you want to keep this activity available throughout the year, you can change the theme of the store (and change the prices to meet their increased skill level) to keep it fresh for the students. The music store or bookstore can have all items of equal value to give practice multiplying decimals.

Make several copies of the paper money and coin sheets. A cash register and basket for carrying items would also help the "realism".

Dining Out (page 47)

One desk or small table with chair should be enough for this activity. Adding a tablecloth, plates, glasses, and cutlery is a nice touch.

Container Capacity (page 49)

If you don't have access to a sink, fill a large bucket or tub with water. Show the students how to scoop up water in their containers and remind them to return the water to the bucket when finished. A few drops of food coloring in the water helps to see it more easily.

Time and Time Again (page 51)

The clock can be student-created from the template or any plastic or real clock. It does not need to be a working clock; it does need moveable hour and minute hands, and, if appropriate for your students' skill level, a "second" hand should be on the clock. Indicate to the students if you want them to include seconds in this activity.

Surface Area of 3D Shapes (page 52)

Using the photocopier, enlarge or shrink the shapes on the template for a greater variety of shape sizes.

Teaching Math with Everyday Manipulatives

Name: _____

Presenting...Perimeters

Measurement

You Will Need:

- assorted 2-dimensional shapes (these can be paper shapes that you or your teacher cut out)
- ruler

Steps:

1. Choose any shape.
2. Use the ruler to measure the sides of the shape.
3. Trace the shape in the table below and record the perimeter underneath it.
4. Repeat with 3 more shapes.

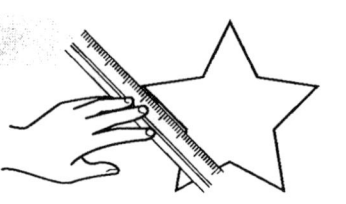

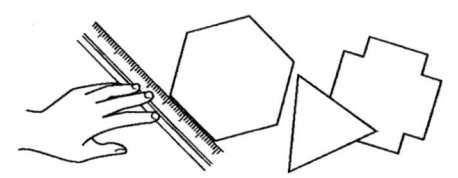

Tip: Instead of using a ruler, you can use the side of a shape with a known length (**Example:** a triangle that has a side of 2 inches or centimeters).

Shape 1	Shape 2
Perimeter: _____	Perimeter: _____
Shape 3	Shape 4
Perimeter: _____	Perimeter: _____

Extension:

Play this game with a partner: Try to be the first one to measure objects with a total combined perimeter of 100 yards (or 100 meters).

© On The Mark Press • S&S Learning Materials

OTM-1134 • SSK1-34 Teaching Math with Everyday Manipulatives

Perfect Perimeters

You Will Need:

- small, straight-edged objects (popsicle stick, straw, paper clip, cubes, etc.)
- larger objects (desk, book, door, etc.)

Steps:

1. Choose larger objects from around the room and estimate the perimeter of whichever unit of measure (small object) you decide.
2. Then, measure the objects and record the answer.

Example:

Object	Measured with	Estimated Perimeter	Actual Perimeter
book	paper clip	16	14
door	drinking straw	12	8

Object	Measured With	Estimated Perimeter	Actual Perimeter

Teaching Math with Everyday Manipulatives

Name: _____

Area and Perimeter

Measurement

You Will Need:

- grid paper (page 77)
- scissors, glue

Steps:

1. Cut out 4 shapes from the grid paper, by cutting along the lines.

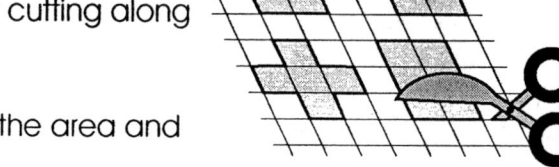

2. Measure, and record in the chart below, the area and perimeter for each shape.

3. Glue the shape onto your paper beside your answers.

Shape 1	Shape 2
Area: _____ Perimeter: _____	Area: _____ Perimeter: _____
Shape 3	Shape 4
Area: _____ Perimeter: _____	Area: _____ Perimeter: _____

Extensions:

Using another piece of grid paper, try making 4 more shapes, with the same area as the 4 you just measured, but with different perimeters!

You may want to make shapes with diagonal lines that divide a square into half!

© On The Mark Press • S&S Learning Materials

Teaching Math with Everyday Manipulatives

Name: _____

Area

Measurement

You Will Need:

- small rectangular or triangular objects or pieces of paper

Steps:

1. Put the first object on the grid paper below and trace it.
2. Estimate the area.
3. Find the actual area and record it.
4. Repeat for different objects.

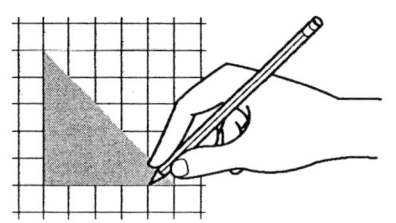

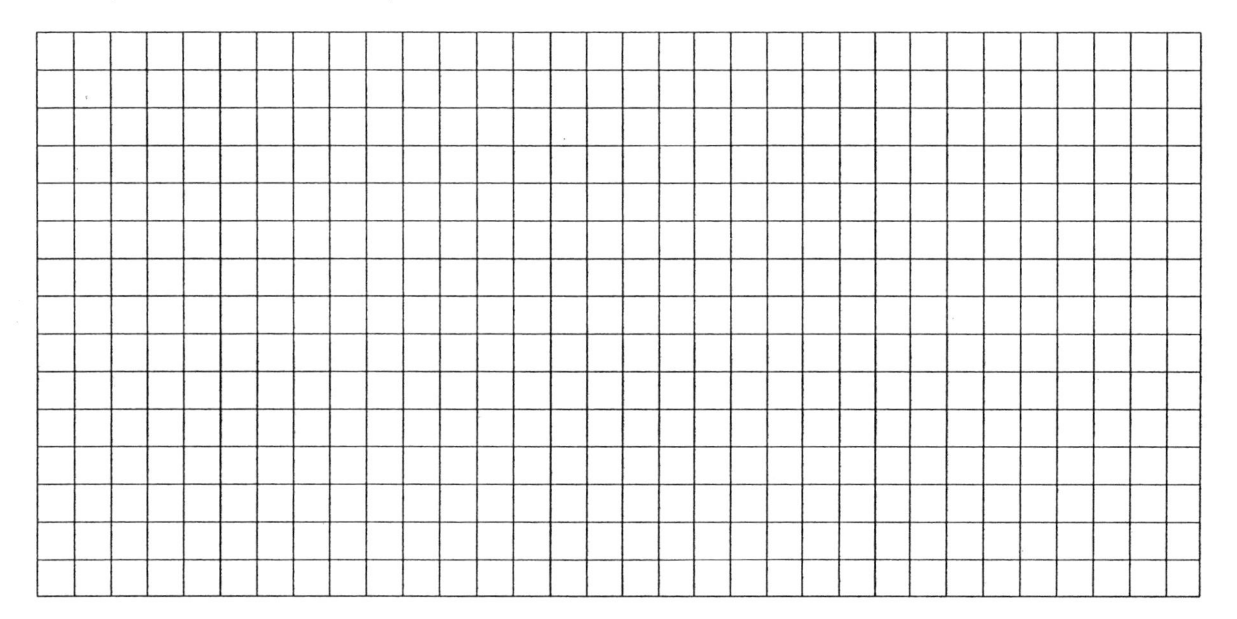

Object 1	Object 2
Estimated area: _____	Estimated area: _____
Actual area: _____	Actual area: _____
Object 3	**Object 4**
Estimated area: _____	Estimated area: _____
Actual area: _____	Actual area: _____

Extension:

If you've mastered rectangles and triangles, try finding the area of some irregular shaped objects!

Shopping Time

You Will Need:
- assorted items with price tags
- "money" (page 78)

Steps:
1. Select 3 items to "buy".
2. Record the cost of each item. Then, add them up to find the total.
3. Count out the money you need to pay for the items.
4. Record the number of dollar bills and coins that give the exact total.

Item	Price	# of $2 coins/bills	# of $1 coins/bills	# of quarters	# of dimes	# of nickels	# of pennies
1	$ _____						
2	$ _____						
3	$ _____						
Total Cost:	$ _____						

Item	Price	# of $2 coins/bills	# of $1 coins/bills	# of quarters	# of dimes	# of nickels	# of pennies
1	$ _____						
2	$ _____						
3	$ _____						
Total Cost:	$ _____						

Teaching Math with Everyday Manipulatives

Name: _____

Dining Out

You Will Need:
- "money" (page 78)

Steps:
1. Choose a theme for a restaurant (fast food, Italian, fine dining, etc.) and fill in the menu below.
2. Decide what you would want to order from the menu. (Select one item from each category.)
4. Record you order, including both the items and their prices. Then, calculate the total. Count out the money you need for the exact total.
5. Give your money to a friend and have them count it to be sure you have the correct amount.

Menu

Appetizers

Item	Price
_____	$ _____
_____	$ _____
_____	$ _____
_____	$ _____

Main Courses

Item	Price
_____	$ _____
_____	$ _____
_____	$ _____
_____	$ _____

Desserts

Item	Price
_____	$ _____
_____	$ _____
_____	$ _____
_____	$ _____

Drinks

Item	Price
_____	$ _____
_____	$ _____
_____	$ _____
_____	$ _____

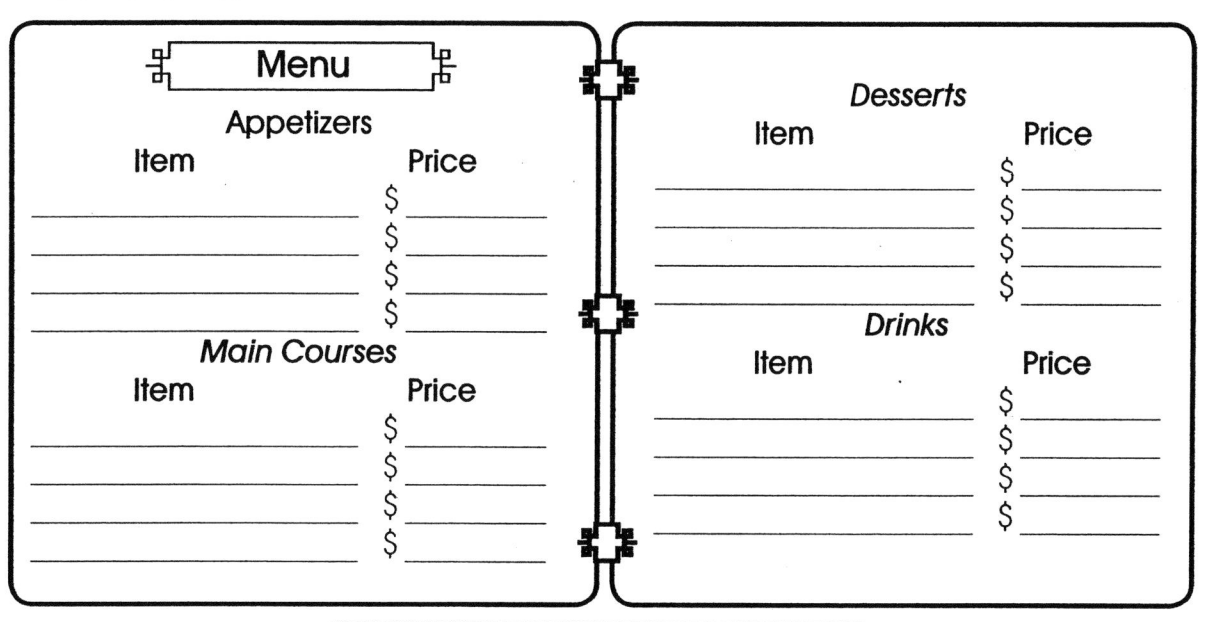

Customer Order

Item	Price
_____	$ _____
_____	$ _____
_____	$ _____
_____	$ _____

Total: $ _____

Extensions:

Add the tax to the bill. Do you know how much tax is added in your state or province? Figure out how much a 20 percent tip is. (The simplest percentage to figure out is 10 percent, and then double that to get 20 percent).

Measuring Mania

You Will Need:

- ruler
- various objects

Steps:

1. Choose an object in the room to measure. Write the item name on the chart.
2. Estimate the length in centimeters or inches. Record your estimate.
4. Using a ruler, measure the actual length. Record.

Example:

Object	Estimate	Actual	Object	Estimate	Actual
book	6 in.		leg		
door	50 in.		easel		
desk			stapler		

Object	Estimate	Actual	Object	Estimate	Actual

Extension:

Convert the actual measurements. (If you measured in centimeters, convert to millimeters or meters. If you measured in inches, convert to feet wherever possible.)

Teaching Math with Everyday Manipulatives

Name: _____

Container Capacity

Measurement

You Will Need:

- 5 containers of different sizes
- measuring cup (small unit of measure)
- water
- masking tape
- marker

Steps:

1. Choose 5 containers.
2. Fill the measuring cup with water and pour into the first container. Repeat until the container is full. Remember to count how many measuring cups you pour.
3. Using the marker, write the measurement (number of cups) on masking tape and tape it to the container.
4. Repeat steps 2 and 3 for the remaining containers.
5. Put the 5 containers in order from smallest capacity to largest capacity.
6. Sketch the shape of the containers and label the capacity of each one below.
7. Empty the water and remove the tape for the next person to use.

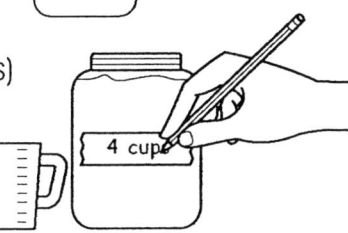

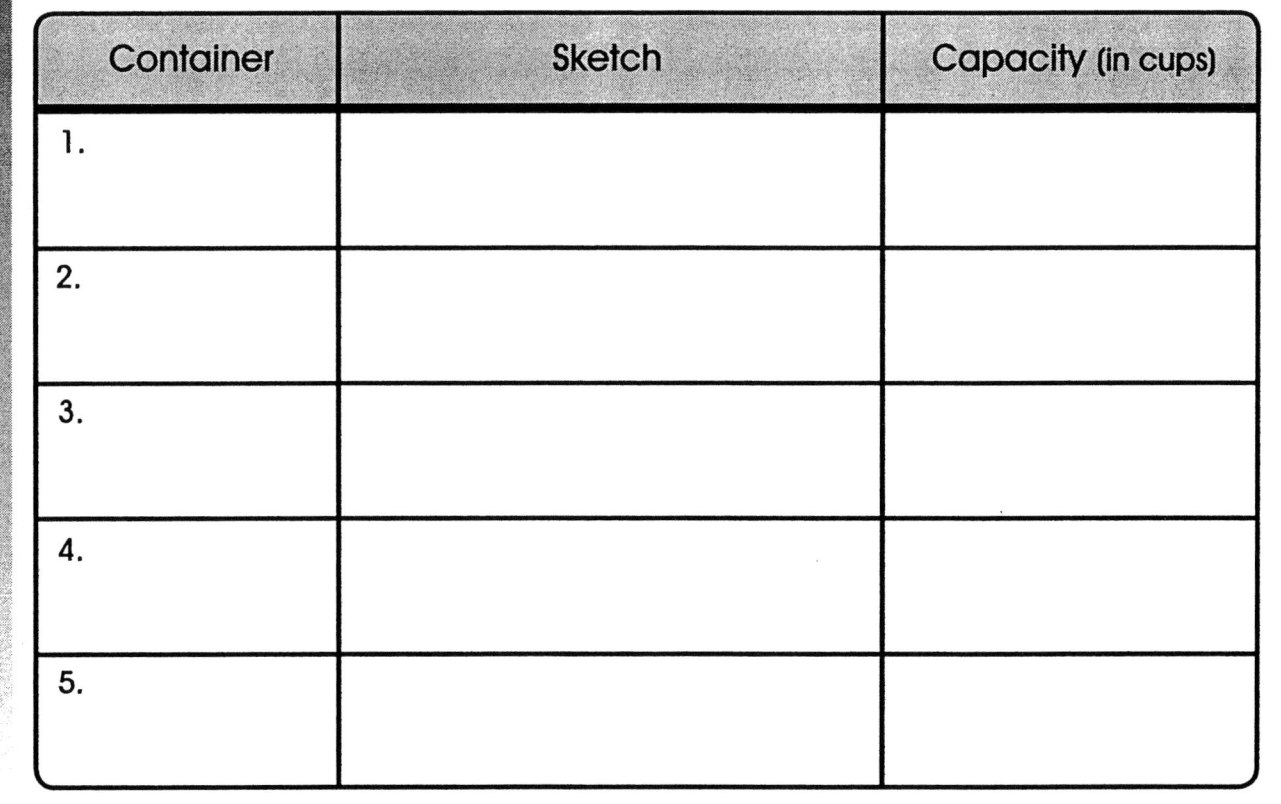

Container	Sketch	Capacity (in cups)
1.		
2.		
3.		
4.		
5.		

Teaching Math with Everyday Manipulatives

Name: _____

Measuring Mass

Measurement

You Will Need:

- objects of varying mass
- balance scales
- weights
- masking tape
- marker

Steps:

1. Choose five objects. Record your estimate of each object.
2. Put the first object on one side of the scales and the weights on the other side until the scale is balanced.
3. Using the marker, write the measurement on masking tape and tape it to the object.
4. Repeat steps 2 to 4 for the remaining objects.
5. Put the objects in order from lightest to heaviest.
6. Record the actual mass.
7. Remove tape and return objects for next person to use.

Example:

Object	pencil	cup	coaster	apple	book
My Estimate (lightest to heaviest)					
Object	pencil	cup	coaster	apple	book
Actual Mass (lightest to heaviest)					

Object					
My Estimate (lightest to heaviest)					
Object					
Actual Mass (lightest to heaviest)					

Extension:

Find the difference in mass between each pair of objects (the difference between the lightest and the second lightest, etc.).

Time and Time Again

You Will Need:

- 2 players
- analog clock for each player (see page 77)

Steps:

1. In the spaces below, write 4 story problems that involves "time spent". Write a title for each story.

   Examples:
   a) Finn has a 35-minute walk to school. School starts at 8:50 a.m. What time does Finn need to leave his house in order to arrive at school on time?
   b) Katie completed the Walkathon in 1 hour, 25 minutes and 13 seconds. She started at 9:27:03 a.m., what time did Katie finish?"
2. Switch worksheets with the other Player. Solve the problems and record the answers.
3. Switch papers again and have the other Player check your work. For each correct solution, the Player gets one point.
4. The Player with the most points wins.

Title: _____

Story Problem: _____
_____
_____
_____
_____

Solution: _____

Title: _____

Story Problem: _____
_____
_____
_____
_____

Solution: _____

Title: _____

Story Problem: _____
_____
_____
_____
_____

Solution: _____

Title: _____

Story Problem: _____
_____
_____
_____
_____

Solution: _____

Your Score: _____

Name: _____

Surface Area of 3D Shapes

You Will Need:

- templates for 3D Shapes (page 79)
- scissors
- ruler

Steps:

1. Choose one of the templates of a 3D shape and cut it out.
2. Choose a template for a different 3D shape that you think has a larger surface area than the first shape you chose.
3. Measure the surface area of each shape. (Tip: Measure the area of each side first. Then, add the area of each side to find the total surface area.)
4. The Player with the shape that has the largest surface area gets a point.

The Player with the most points after 6 rounds is the winner.

Shape 1 Sketch (Largest Area)	Shape 2 Sketch (Smallest Area)	Actual Area (Shape 1)	Actual Area (Shape 2)	Were my area estimates correct?
1.				
2.				
3.				
4.				
5.				

Your Sore: _____

Teaching Math with Everyday Manipulatives

Data & Probability

Overview

Data and probability is the study of information about the world by collecting data and using the information to answer questions and make judgments based on experience. Manipulatives should be used to help students collect and represent data. The activities suggested in this book should, with regular practise over time, allow students to develop stronger data and probability skills.

The NCTM Standards for the Junior Grade levels suggest that students should:

- design investigations to address a question and consider how data-collection methods affect the nature of the data set;
- collect data using observations, surveys, and experiments;
- represent data using tables and graphs such as line plots, bar graphs, and line graphs;
- recognize the differences in representing categorical and numerical data;
- describe the shape and important features of a set of data and compare related data sets, with an emphasis on how the data are distributed;
- use measures of center, focusing on the median, and understand what each does and does not indicate about the data set;
- compare different representations of the same data and evaluate how well each representation shows important aspects of the data;
- propose and justify conclusions and predictions that are based on data and design studies to further investigate the conclusions or predictions;
- describe events as likely or unlikely and discuss the degree of likelihood using such words as certain, equally likely, and impossible;
- predict the probability of outcomes of simple experiments and test the predictions;
- understand that the measure of the likelihood of an event can be represented by a number from 0 to 1.

Teacher Preparation Notes:

Probability Picks (page 62)

Put out (or set guidelines) that are suitable for your students' skill level. Early Junior students may do best with less objects to start with and 2 or 3 different colors/designs, etc. As students progress, they may be able to expand the total number of objects and the number of "different" items. For example, younger students may use 15 coins (10 pennies and 5 nickels) or 15 buttons (5 white, 5 black, and 5 blue). Older students may use a larger number of objects with more variations.

Teaching Math with Everyday Manipulatives

Name: _____

Cool Cuisenaire Rods

Data & Probability

You Will Need:

- stiff paper of ten different colors (see page 80)
- scissors
- Ziplock bag with your name on it

Steps:

1. Carefully trace and cut out each of the rectangles and color them according to their label.
2. Label them all with a fraction. For example the smallest, white ones should all be labeled 1/10.
3. Discover the relationships between the rods. For example, 10 white rods are equal to one orange rod.
5. Write 5 equivalent fractions based on what you have learned about the relationships, for example, 10/10 = 1.

Example:

2/4 = 1/2

6. Store these in the baggie.

Probability Practice

You Will Need:

- circular object, about 10 centimeters (4 inches) in diameter (lid from a jar or plastic container, small paper plate, etc.)
- blank paper
- scissors
- ruler
- paperclip

Steps:

1. Trace and cut out 4 circles.
2. Using a ruler, divide the circles into sections labeled A and B so that:
   a) In 100 spins it will likely land on A 30 times.
   b) In 100 spins it will likely land on A 60 times.
   c) In 100 spins it will likely land on A 75 times.
   d) In 100 spins it will likely land on A 90 times.
3. Now, hold the paperclip with a pencil in the middle of the circle and spin it 100 times.
4. For each circle, make a sketch of how you divided it, and record how many times the paperclip actually did land on A.

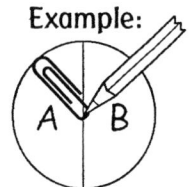

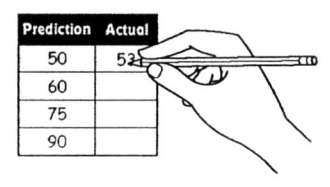

Circle	Sketch	Prediction – In 100 spins the paperclip will land on A:	Actual – In 100 spins the paperclip landed on A:
1.		30 times	_____ times
2.		60 times	_____ times
3.		75 times	_____ times
4.		90 times	_____ times

Extension:

1. Divide the circles into 3 or 4 sections, labeled, A, B, C and D.
2. Exchange them with a friend and have them predict how often the spinner will land on each of the letters in 100 spins.
3. Record the actual results.

Teaching Math with Everyday Manipulatives

Name: _____

Dice Tally

Data & Probability

You Will Need:

- 2 or 3 die

Steps:

1. Take turns rolling the die.

2. Record (with a check mark) each time a sum is rolled. Record your results in the tally sheet below. (Sums will continue to 12 if two die are used, and 18 if three die are used).

3. The first Player to roll the same sum 10 times is the Winner.

Tally Sheet

Sum	Tally ✓✓✓✓✓✓✓✓✓✓	Sum	Tally ✓✓✓✓✓✓✓✓✓✓
1		10	
2		11	
3		12	
4		13	
5		14	
6		15	
7		16	
8		17	
9		18	

Double Probability

You Will Need:

- circular object, about 10 centimeters (4 inches) in diameter (lid from a jar or plastic container, small paper plate, etc.)
- blank paper
- scissors
- ruler
- paperclip

Steps:

1. Trace and cut out 2 circles.
2. Divide one circle into 3 sections (any size) labeled A, B and C. Divide the other circle into 3 sections labeled 1, 2, and 3.
3. In the chart below, list all possible combinations of outcomes if both spinners were spun (for example, A1, B1, etc.). There will be 9 combinations.
4. Based on the size of the different sections, circle the combination that you think will happen the most often. Underline the combination that you think will happen the least often.
5. Spin both spinners and keep a tally record (with check marks) of how often each combination is spun.
6. After 50 spins check to see if your predictions were correct.

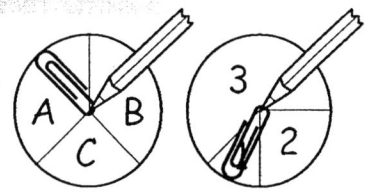

Tally Sheet

Combination	Tally (✓)

Teaching Math with Everyday Manipulatives

Name: _____

Predicting with Data

Data & Probability

You Will Need:

- stopwatch (or a clock or watch with a second hand)

Steps:

1. Choose a simple, repetitive task such as putting pennies into a container one at a time, printing your name, jumping jacks, etc.
2. Player 1 does the task while Player 2 times them.
3. When Player 1 has done the task 5 times, Player 2 says, "Stop" and records, in the data chart below, how many seconds it took.
4. Player 1 keeps doing the task with Player 2 recording the times. When Player 1 has done the task a total of 25 times, the Players switch roles.
6. Each Player then records their data on the graph. (Add the seconds that match your time.)
7. Use the graph to predict how many seconds it would take to do the task 50 times and 100 times.

Data Chart – Task:

Task Time in Seconds	(# Times Task is Done) 5 10 15 20 25	50 (Prediction)	100 (Prediction)
100			
90			
80			
70			
60			
50			
40			
30			
20			
10			
0			

Temperature Data

You Will Need:

- thermometer

Steps:

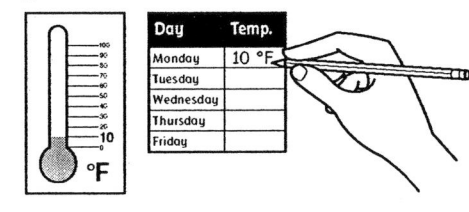

1. Measure and record the outside temperature at the same time of day, each school day for one month (30 days).
2. At the end of the month, display your data in the bar graph, line graph and pie chart below.
3. Write down 10 questions about your data. (**Examples:** Which day was the coldest? What was the mean (average) temperature? What was the median (middle) temperature? What was the mode (most common) temperature?)
4. Use your graphs to find the answers. Make a note of which graph you are using to answer each question.

Bar Graph

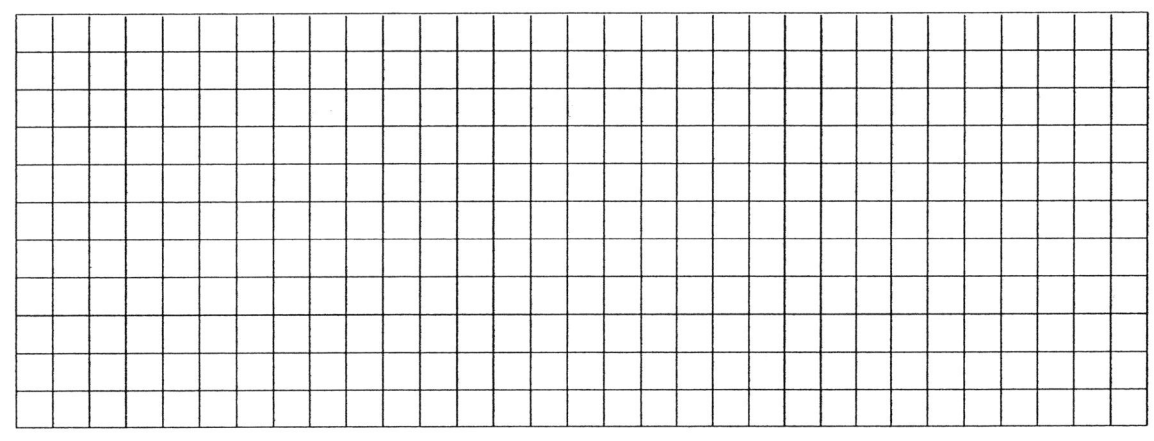

Line Graph

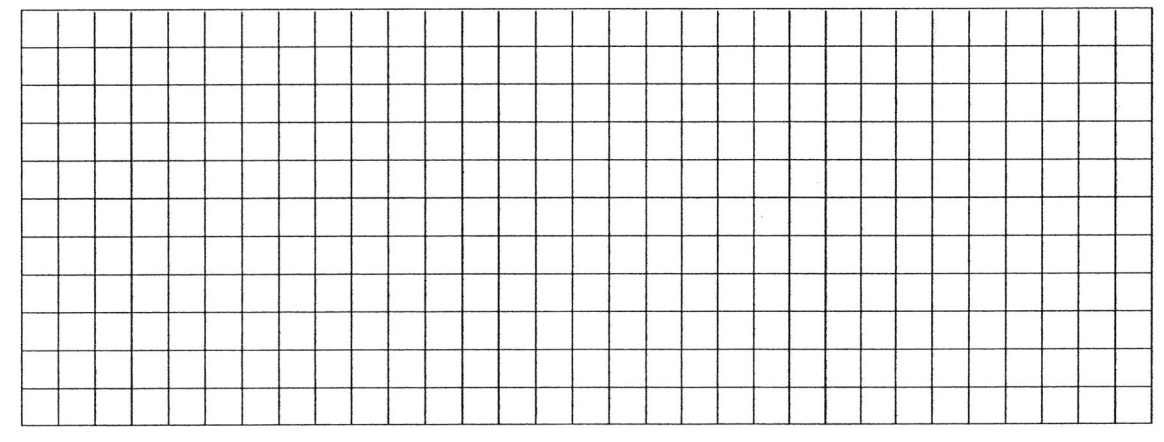

Teaching Math with Everyday Manipulatives

Name: _____

Temperature Data

Data & Probability

Pie Chart

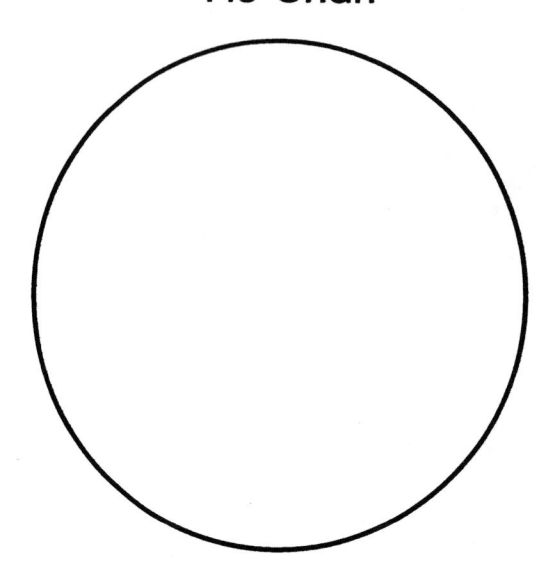

Question	Answer	Graph Used to Solve
1.		
2.		
3.		
4.		
5.		
6.		
7.		
8.		
9.		
10.		

Teaching Math with Everyday Manipulatives

Name: _____

Forward or Stop

You Will Need:

- 2 counters of different colors (button, bean, tile, etc.), one for each player
- dice

0 --------------------- 1 --------------------- 2 --------------------- 3

Steps:

1. Both Players start at 0 on the number line above.
2. Player 1 rolls the dice. If it is even, they move their counter forward one space. If it is odd, they do not move. Player 1 rolls the dice two more times, and for each roll, moves their counter forward for even, or stops for odd.
3. After 3 rolls, Player 2 rolls the dice 3 times, and moves their counter on the number line.
4. For each roll record whether it is odd or even in the chart below, and write which number on the line you ended up on.
5. Each Player has a total of ten turns.
6. Complete the chart below by putting tally marks in the proper column.

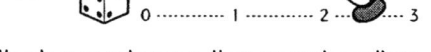

Turn	Roll 1 Odd Even	Roll 2 Odd Even	Roll 3 Odd Even	Number Line Total 0 1 2 3
1				
2				
3				
4				
5				
6				
7				
8				
9				
10				

Position at End of Turn

7. Answer the following questions:

   Which number did you land on the most? _____
   Which number did you land on the least? _____
   What is the probability of landing on: 0? _____ 1? _____ 2? _____ 3? _____
   What is the probability of landing on a number higher than 1? _____
   If you rolled the dice 3 times each turn, for 100 turns, what is the probability of ending up on: 0? _____ 1? _____ 2? _____ 3? _____

Teaching Math with Everyday Manipulatives

Name: _____

Probability Picks

You Will Need:

- objects
- container

Steps:

1. Put some objects into a container. Record below how many objects there are in total, and how many of each different object there are. (For example, "There are 30 buttons. 10 are purple; 15 are silver; 5 are yellow.")
2. Guess the probability of choosing 2 certain objects in 6 tries. (For example, "I think there is a 75% chance of choosing 2 silver buttons" or "I think there is a 25% chance of choosing a yellow and purple button".)
3. Then, reach into the container (without looking) and pick 2 objects. Record the results in the chart, and repeat for a total of 6 times.

How many objects are there in total? _____

How many of each is there? _____
_____

Turn	Guess	Objects Pulled from Jar
1		
2		
3		
4		
5		
6		

4. Answer the following questions.

   Why did you make the prediction that you did? _____

   Was your guess close? Why or why not? _____

   Did you get more accurate at guessing? _____

   Do you think it would have made a difference if you had picked 100 times instead of 10? Why? _____

Teaching Math with Everyday Manipulatives

Name: _____

Spinning Probabilities

You Will Need:

- circle or small paper plate
- paperclip (to use as a spinner)

Steps:

1. Write 4 criteria for your spinner using "more likely" or "less likely" in each.
   Examples: I will more likely spin a 3 than a 4. I will less likely spin a 1 or 2 than 3 or higher.
2. Create a spinner that fits all your criteria.
3. When your spinner is complete, spin the paperclip around a pencil tip 20 times and record the results. Include a sketch of your spinner.

1. I will more likely spin a 3 than a 4

My Criteria:

1. _____
2. _____
3. _____
4. _____

Sketch	Spin	Result	Spin	Result
	1		6	
	2		7	
	3		8	
	4		9	
	5		10	

Did the results of the spinning match your criteria? _____

© On The Mark Press • S&S Learning Materials

Teaching Math with Everyday Manipulatives

Name: _____

Rolling for Outcomes

Data & Probability

You Will Need:

- 10 counters (buttons, coins, etc.) for each Player (a different color or kind for each player)
- 2 die

2--------3--------4--------5--------6--------7--------8--------9--------10--------11--------12

Steps:

1. Each Player places their counters next to any of the numbers on the number line above. One Player should place their counters above the number and the other Player should place their's below the number.
2. Player 1 rolls both die and adds the two numbers together. If you have a counter at that number, remove it. (If you have more than one counter at that number, just remove one.) Record the result in the chart.
3. Player 2 rolls and removes a counter, if possible, and records the result.
4. The play continues until one Player has removed all their counters.

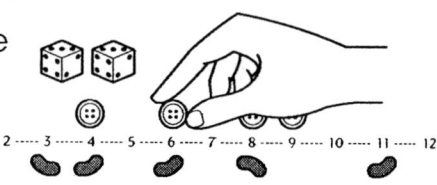

Turn	Sum of Dice	Action	Turn	Sum of Dice	Action
1			9		
2			10		
3			11		
4			12		
5			13		
6			14		
7			15		
8			16		

Extension:

1. Discuss how you chose to place your counters.
2. What would you do differently next time to improve your chances of removing all your counters first?

© On The Mark Press • S&S Learning Materials

OTM-1134 • SSK1-34 Teaching Math with Everyday Manipulatives

Teaching Math with Everyday Manipulatives

Algebra

Overview:

Algebra is the study of the relationships between quantities, the use of symbols and the study of change. Manipulatives should be used to help students focus on looking for and making mathematical observations and resulting predictions with words, symbols and math sentences. The activities suggested in this book should, with regular practice over time, allow students to develop stronger algebra skills.

The NCTM Standards for the Junior Grade levels suggest that students should:

- describe, extend, and make generalizations about geometric and numeric patterns;
- represent and analyze patterns and functions, using words, tables, and graphs;
- identify such properties as commutativity, associativity, and distributivity and use them to compute with whole numbers;
- represent the idea of a variable as an unknown quantity using a letter or a symbol;
- express mathematical relationships using equations;
- model problem situations with objects and use representations such as graphs, tables, and equations to draw conclusions;
- investigate how a change in one variable relates to a change in a second variable;
- identify and describe situations with constant or varying rates of change and compare them.

Teacher Preparation Notes:

Comparing Graphs (page 70)

Prepare a variety of rectangles that will exactly fit onto the grid paper (6x7 or 9x5, etc.). If your students are ready for irregular shapes, you can prepare inexact shapes for this activity.

Perfect Problem Solvers (page 71)

Change the objects throughout the year to encourage different types of questions. Plastic money, or paper cut outs of currency other than pennies will prompt different money and decimal related questions. Small dollhouse type people or paper cutouts of a variety of people shapes could be used for logic type questions (e.g., Sierra is shorter than Tyra. Tyra is taller than Madison. Cole is the shortest. Madison is shorter than Sierra. Put the four people in order of height.). Both problem solving and logic problems are challenging to create, and by making their own problems, the students will further their understanding of what information is imperative and what is extraneous.

Teaching Math with Everyday Manipulatives

Name: _____

Graphing a Line Plot

Algebra

You Will Need:

- small objects (pennies, buttons, dried beans, etc.)
- ruler

Steps:

1. Ask a classmate one of the following questions, and record the data on a separate sheet of paper:
   How much have you grown each grade you've been in school?
   How many baby teeth have you lost each grade?
   How many candy bars have you eaten each month this year?
2. Label the graph axes below so that the numbers that you have in your data will fit.
3. Graph your results on the graph using the small objects.
4. Remove the objects from the line plot one at a time and replace them with an X. Use your ruler to connect the Xs in a line.
5. Label your line plot.

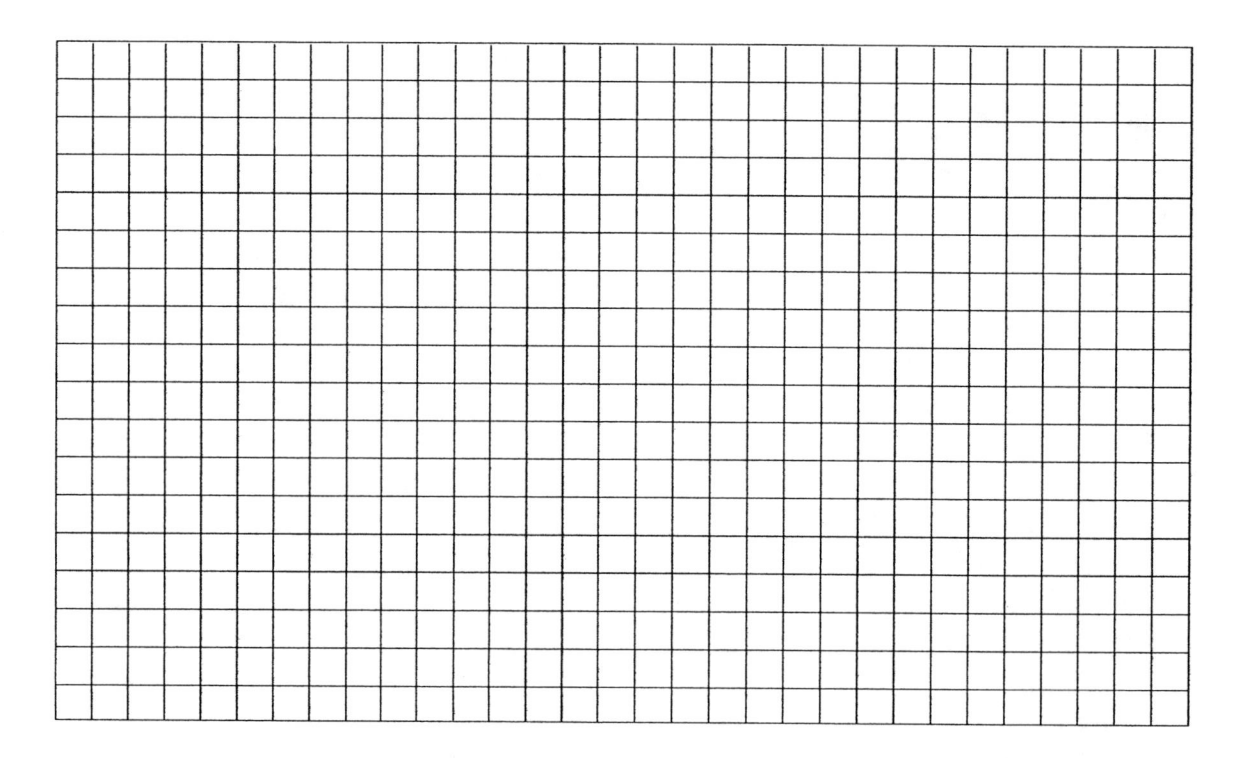

Name: _____

Growth Patterns

You Will Need:

- 2 different kinds of small objects, many of each (dried beans and pennies, or red buttons and yellow buttons, etc.)

Steps:

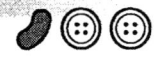

1. Start a growth pattern using the 2 different kinds of objects.

2. Add to the pattern until it is repeated 5 times.

3. Fill in the chart to record the number of each item after each repetition.

Repetition Number	Total Number of _____	Total Number of _____
To Begin		
2		
3		
4		
5		

Extensions:

1. Write a rule to describe how many of one object you would need if you know how many of the other you are using. In the above example, the rule is *multiply the number of beans by 2 to get the number of buttons.*
2. Use grid or graph paper to plot the data.
3. Use 3 different objects. Use 4 different objects.

© On The Mark Press • S&S Learning Materials 67 OTM-1134 • SSK1-34 Teaching Math with Everyday Manipulatives

Teaching Math with Everyday Manipulatives

Name: _____

Munching Numbers

You Will Need:

- 12 index cards (6 for each player)
- 2 blue markers
- 2 Ziploc bags ("Muncher")
- 2 red markers

Steps:

1. Each Player thinks of a secret rule (for example, multiply by 3).
2. Using the blue marker, write a number on one side of the index card (example: 4).
3. Turn the card over. Apply the secret rule to the number on the front of the card and, using the red marker, write the new number on the back of the index card (example: 12).
4. Each Player makes 3 cards, each with a different number on the front side. Using the same secret rule, write the number for the back side. Put the 3 cards into the "Muncher" and trade with the other Player.
5. Each Player will try to guess the secret rule. Look at the blue number and think about what the "Muncher" did to it to make the red number.
6. When you think you have figured out the secret rule, make 3 more cards using that rule.
7. Fill in the chart with the blue and red numbers on all 6 cards, and write out the number sentence for each card that shows the secret rule.

   Example: **Blue Number**   **Red Number**   **Number Sentence**

   Card 1   4   12   <u>4 x 3 = 12</u>

8. Leave the Ziploc bags for others to figure out the rule of your "Muncher".

	Blue Number	Red Number	Number Sentence
Card 1			___ ___ = ___
Card 2			___ ___ = ___
Card 3			___ ___ = ___
Card 4			___ ___ = ___
Card 5			___ ___ = ___
Card 6			___ ___ = ___

Extensions:

Make a 2-step "Muncher"! Can you figure out the 2-step secret rule for this "Muncher"?

	Blue Number	Red Number	Number Sentence
Card 1	3	7	3 ___ ___ = 7
Card 2	5	11	5 ___ ___ = 11
Card 3	8	17	8 ___ ___ = 17

(The secret rule is $n \times 2 + 1$)

Teaching Math with Everyday Manipulatives

Name: _____

Algebra

You Will Need:

- 2 Players

Steps:

1. Player 1 thinks of a secret rule. Beginners at this game may use a rule such as "add the numbers". Advanced Players may use a rule such as "divide the numbers and subtract 3".
2. Write down 3 numbers that fit your secret rule.
   In the beginner example, the numbers may be:

   3   3   6 (because 3 + 3 = 6)

   In the advanced example, the numbers may be:

   25   5   2 (because 25 : 5 – 3 = 2)
3. Player 2 can guess the rule at any time, or ask for more groups of 3 numbers to see how the first 2 numbers relate to the third number.
4. When Player 2 correctly guesses the secret rule, he or she writes the number sentence that shows the secret rule for each group on numbers.
5. Switch roles.

Player 1: _____   Player 2: _____

3 Numbers	Number Sentence	What is the Secret Rule?
___ ___ ___	_____ = ___	_____
___ ___ ___	_____ = ___	_____
___ ___ ___	_____ = ___	_____
___ ___ ___	_____ = ___	_____
___ ___ ___	_____ = ___	_____
___ ___ ___	_____ = ___	_____

© On The Mark Press • S&S Learning Materials

Teaching Math with Everyday Manipulatives

Name: _____

Comparing Graphs

Algebra

You Will Need:

- 2-dimensional paper shapes (different sizes and shapes)
- grid paper

Steps:

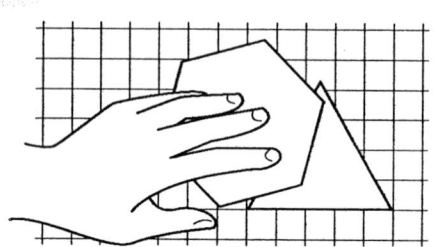

1. Choose a shape.
2. Look at the shapes that are left and choose a second shape that you think has a greater area. Make a sketch of both shapes in the chart below.
3. Put both shapes on the grid paper and try to the first shape.
4. Then, in the chart, calculate the area of each shape and answer "Yes" or "No" to the question, "Was your prediction correct?"
5. Repeat steps 1 to 4 four more times with different shapes.

Predicted Area		Calculation of Actual Area		Was Your Prediction Correct?
Shape 1 Sketch (Smallest area)	Shape 2 Sketch (Greatest area)	Shape 1	Shape 2	

© On The Mark Press • S&S Learning Materials

OTM-1134 • SSK1-34 Teaching Math with Everyday Manipulatives

Teaching Math with Everyday Manipulatives

Name: _____

Perfect Problem Solvers

Algebra

You Will Need:

- about a hundred small objects (buttons, pennies, dried beans)
- a copy of this page for each Player
- 2 Players

Steps:

1. Player 1 writes 3 different problem-solving questions in the chart below that can be solved using the objects.

   Example:
   Malcolm sewed 6 buttons on each of 7 sweaters. How many buttons did Malcolm use?

2. Trade pages with the other Player. Take turns using the objects to show how you are solving the problem that the other Player wrote. Explain to the other Player how you are solving the problem. Record your solution in the chart.

   Example:
   Make 7 piles of 6 buttons. Count the buttons for the total number of buttons used. Total = 42

   Note: Each Player who created the question must be prepared to show how to solve the problem, using the objects.

Problem	Solution
1.	
2.	
3.	

© On The Mark Press • S&S Learning Materials

OTM-1134 • SSK1-34 Teaching Math with Everyday Manipulatives

Teaching Math with Everyday Manipulatives

Name: _____

Stem and Leaf Plots

Algebra

Steps:

1. Ask 10 people to pick a number between 10 and 50.

2. Record their answers in the stem and leaf graph below.

   To make a stem and leaf graph, consider each stem to be the first digit in a 2-digit number, or the 'ten' place value. For example, the 1 in 10, the 2 in 20, and so on. Write the second digit for the numbers in the leaf box in a row.

   For example, for 10, write a 0 in the leaf box beside the stem 1. For 25, write a 5 beside the stem 2.

Numbers Picked Between 10 and 50

Stem	Leaf									
1										
2										
3										
4										
5										

3. Answer the following questions:

   What was the highest answer? _____

   What was the lowest answer? _____

   What was the mean number? _____

   What was the median number? _____

   Was there a number that was more commonly chosen than any other? _____

Extension:

Ask people to chose a 3- or 4-digit number or a decimal. Always give them a range of about 30 or 40 numbers to choose from.

Fun with Polygons

Algebra

You Will Need:

- Polygons for each Player (different shapes and sizes)
- 2 Players

Steps:

1. Each Player takes some polygons (the fewer you have, the easier this game is; agree on a number together).

2. Without letting the other Player see, arrange your polygons in the space below to make a new shape.

3. Trace the outline of the entire shape.

4. Switch papers and see who can be the first Player to recreate the shape that the other Player outlined. The same polygons do not necessarily need to be used, as long as the shape comes out the same.

Teaching Math with Everyday Manipulatives

Name: _____

Slide and Switch

Algebra

You Will Need:

- 4 buttons of one color, 4 buttons of another color (or coins, etc.)

Steps:

1. In each row, put one button to the left of the middle circle and one button of the other color to the right of the middle circle. (All 8 buttons should be displayed, with 2 on each row.)

2. The object is to switch all the buttons to the other side.

3. **Rules:** – Move a button one circle at a time to an adjacent empty circle, or jump over 1 button to an empty circle.
   – Buttons that start on the left can only move to the right, up or down, or diagonally.
   – Buttons that start on the right can only move to the left, up or down, or diagonally.
   – If you are left without a legitimate move, you are out.

4. Player 1 moves and Player 2 records the number of moves. Then, switch roles. The Player who completes the switch with the lowest number of moves is the winner.

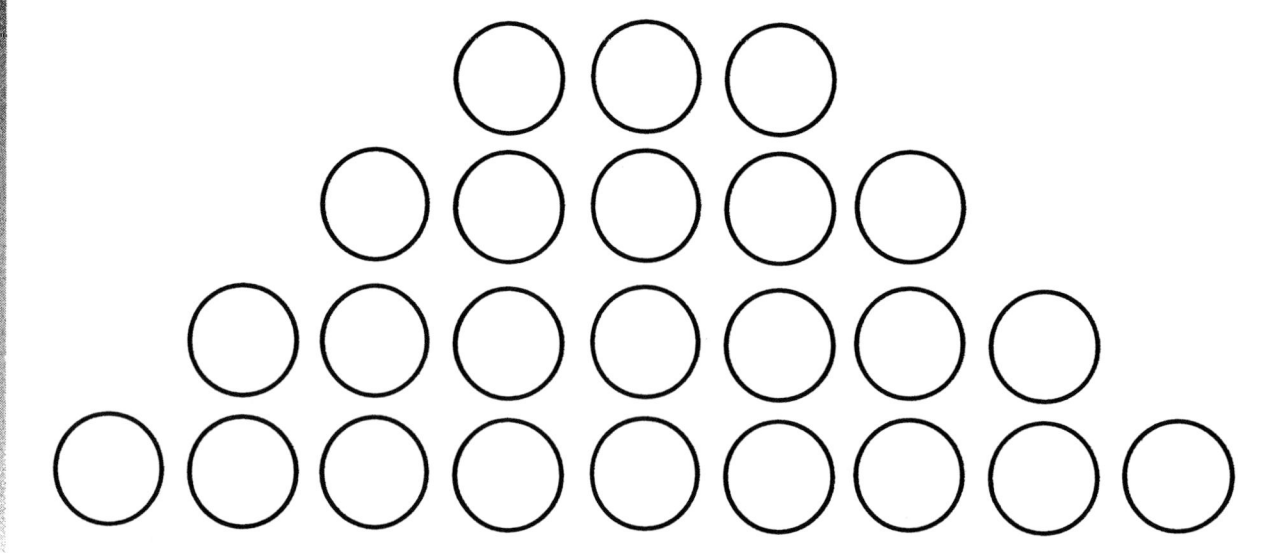

Extension:

When you have mastered the 2-button switch, try 4, 6, or 8 buttons! The middle circle always starts out empty.

Teaching Math with Everyday Manipulatives

Name: _____

Pattern Blocks

Algebra

You Will Need:
- Pattern Blocks (see page 76)

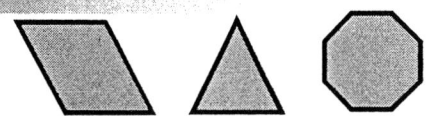

Steps:

1. Each Player determines a value for the shapes. (**Hint:** Secretly write them down, so that you don't forget!)

   For example, you might use something like this:

Shape Type – Equivalent Area		Shape Type – Equivalent Area	
Triangle	1 unit	Square	2 units
Rhombus	2 units	Rhombus	4 units
Trapezoid	3 units	Hexagon	6 units

   Note: 6 triangles have the same area as 1 hexagon, so the hexagon is 6 times the value as the triangle. You need to keep these ratios the same, even when using different values (for example, the triangle could be 1/6 if the hexagon is 1). You don't need to use all the shapes.

2. Make up 3 equations, using the shapes.

   Example: ▱ + ☐ = 1

3. Switch equations with the other Player. Each Player must then figure out the value of the shapes used in the equations.

   In the example given, the rhombus has a value of 1/2 and the square has a value of 1/2.

Equation	What are the values of the shapes?

© On The Mark Press • S&S Learning Materials   75   OTM-1134 • SSK1-34 Teaching Math with Everyday Manipulatives

Teaching Math with Everyday Manipulatives

Base Ten Blocks

1   10

100   1000

Pattern Blocks

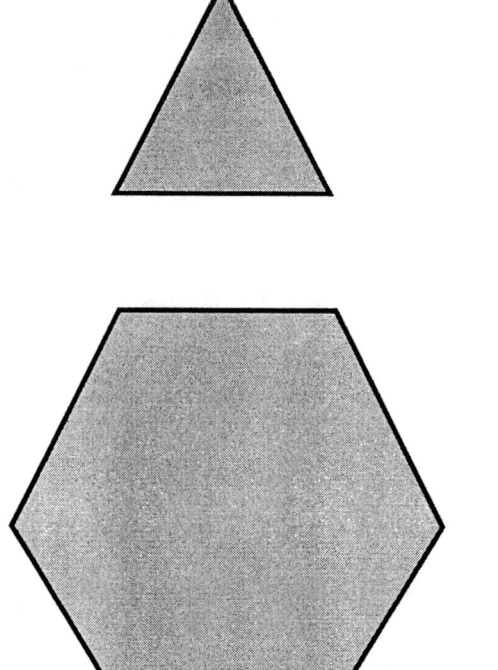

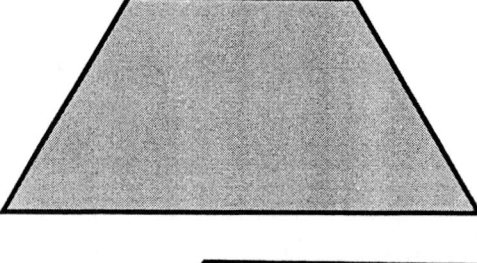

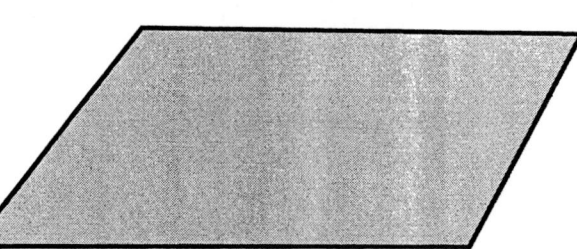

Teaching Math with Everyday Manipulatives

Clock Pattern

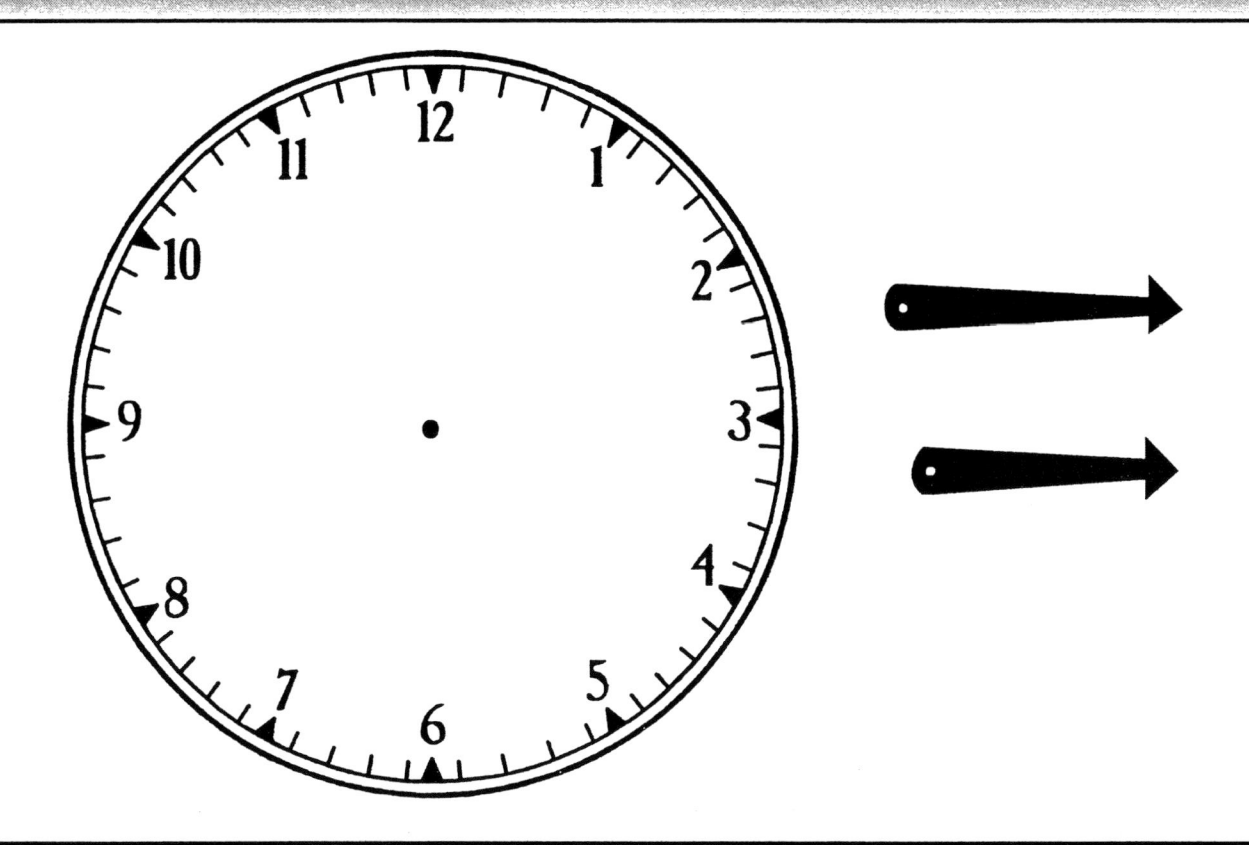

Grid (1 cm)

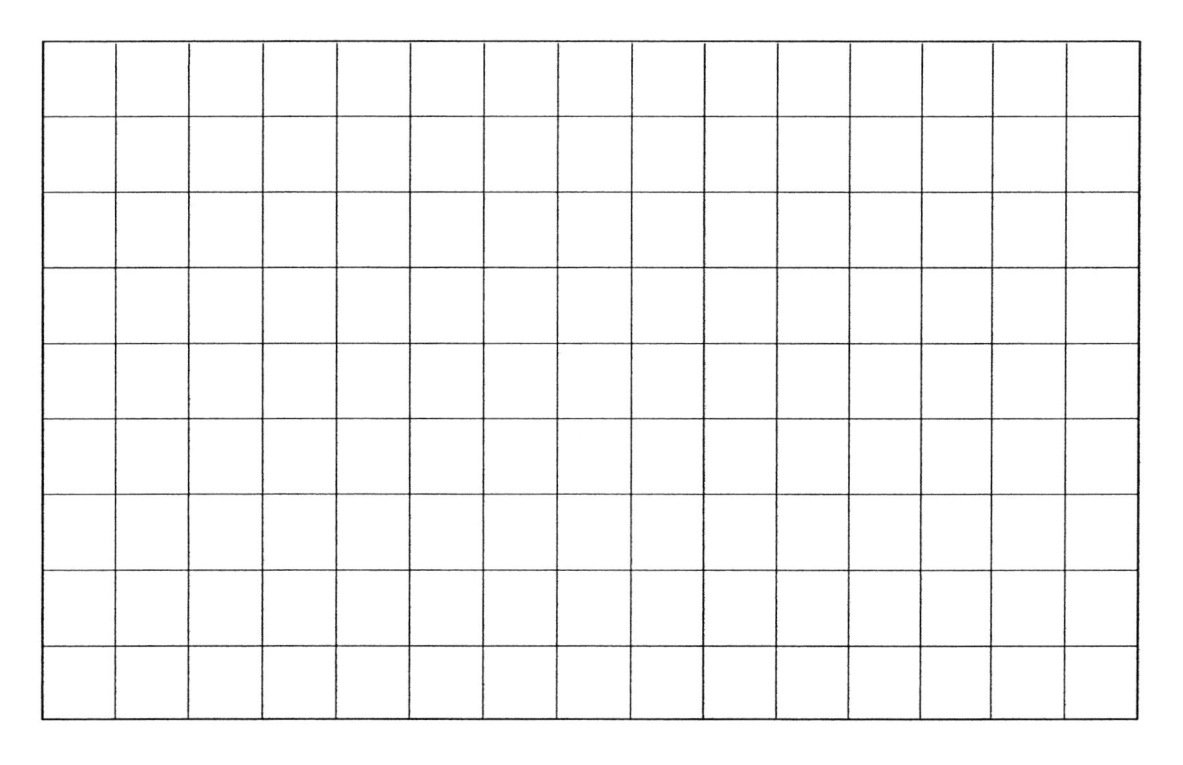

Teaching Math with Everyday Manipulatives

Money (U.S.)

Money (Canadian)

Teaching Math with Everyday Manipulatives

Geometric Shapes

Teaching Math with Everyday Manipulatives

Cuisenaire Rods

white — 1 cm

red — 2 cm

light green — 3 cm

purple — 4 cm

yellow — 5 cm

orange — 10 cm

blue — 9 cm

brown — 8 cm

black — 7 cm

dark green — 6 cm

Venn Diagram

Publication Listing

See Dealer or
www.sslearning.com
For Pricing
1-800-463-6367

Code #	Title and Grade
SSC1-12	A Time of Plenty Gr. 2
SSN1-92	Abel's Island NS Gr. 4-6
SSF1-16	Aboriginal Peoples of Canada Gr. 7-8
SSK1-31	Addition & Subtraction Drills Gr. 1-3
SSK1-28	Addition Drills Gr. 1-3
SSY1-04	Addition Gr. 1-3
SSN1-174	Adv. of Huckle Berry Finn NS Gr. 7-8
SSB1-63	African Animals Gr. 4-6
SSB1-29	All About Bears Gr. 1-2
SSF1-08	All About Boats Gr. 2-3
SSJ1-02	All About Canada Gr. 2
SSB1-54	All About Cattle Gr. 4-6
SSN1-10	All About Colours Gr. P-1
SSB1-93	All About Dinosaurs Gr. 2
SSN1-14	All About Dragons Gr. 3-5
SSB1-07	All About Elephants Gr. 3-4
SSB1-68	All About Fish Gr. 4-6
SSN1-39	All About Giants Gr. 2-3
SSH1-15	All About Jobs Gr. 1-3
SSH1-05	All About Me Gr. 1
SSA1-02	All About Mexico Gr. 4-6
SSR1-28	All About Nouns Gr. 5-7
SSF1-09	All About Planes Gr. 2-3
SSB1-33	All About Plants Gr. 2-3
SSR1-29	All About Pronouns Gr. 5-7
SSB1-12	All About Rabbits Gr. 2-3
SSB1-58	All About Spiders Gr. 4-6
SSA1-03	All About the Desert Gr. 4-6
SSA1-04	All About the Ocean Gr. 5-7
SSZ1-01	All About the Olympics Gr. 2-4
SSB1-49	All About the Sea Gr. 4-6
SSK1-06	All About Time Gr. 4-6
SSF1-07	All About Trains Gr. 2-3
SSH1-18	All About Transportation Gr. 2
SSB1-01	All About Trees Gr. 4-6
SSB1-61	All About Weather Gr. 7-8
SSB1-06	All About Whales Gr. 3-4
SSPC-26	All Kinds of Clocks B/W Pictures
SSB1-110	All Kinds of Structures Gr. 1
SSH1-19	All Kinds of Vehicles Gr. 3
SSF1-01	Amazing Aztecs Gr. 4-6
SSB1-92	Amazing Earthworms Gr. 2-3
SSJ1-50	Amazing Facts in Cdn History Gr. 4-6
SSB1-32	Amazing Insects Gr. 4-6
SSN1-132	Amelia Bedelia–Camping NS 1-3
SSN1-68	Amelia Bedelia NS 1-3
SSN1-155	Amelia Bedelia-Surprise Shower NS 1-3
SSA1-13	America The Beautiful Gr. 4-6
SSN1-57	Amish Adventure NS 7-8
SSF1-02	Ancient China Gr. 4-6
SSF1-18	Ancient Egypt Gr. 4-6
SSF1-21	Ancient Greece Gr. 4-6
SSF1-19	Ancient Rome Gr. 4-6
SSQ1-06	Animal Town – Big Book Pkg 1-3
SSQ1-02	Animals Prepare Winter – Big Book Pkg 1-3
SSN1-150	Animorphs the Invasion NS 4-6
SSN1-53	Anne of Green Gables NS 7-8
SSB1-40	Apple Celebration Gr. 4-6
SSB1-04	Apple Mania Gr. 2-3
SSB1-38	Apples are the Greatest Gr. P-K
SSB1-59	Arctic Animals Gr. 4-6
SSN1-162	Arnold Lobel Author Study Gr. 2-3
SSPC-22	Australia B/W Pictures
SSA1-05	Australia Gr. 5-8
SSM1-03	Autumn in the Woodlot Gr. 2-3
SSM1-08	Autumn Wonders Gr. 1
SSN1-41	Baby Sister for Frances NS 1-3
SSPC-19	Back to School B/W Pictures
SSC1-33	Back to School Gr. 2-3
SSN1-224	Banner in the Sky NS 7-8
SSN1-36	Bargain for Frances NS 1-3
SSB1-82	Bats Gr. 4-6
SSN1-71	BB – Drug Free Zone NS Gr. 1-3
SSN1-88	BB – In the Freaky House NS 1-3
SSN1-78	BB – Media Madness NS 1-3
SSN1-69	BB – Wheelchair Commando NS 1-3
SSN1-119	Be a Perfect Person-3 Days NS 4-6
SSC1-15	Be My Valentine Gr. 1
SSD1-01	Be Safe Not Sorry Gr. P-1
SSN1-09	Bear Tales Gr. 2-4
SSB1-28	Bears Gr. 4-6
SSN1-202	Bears in Literature Gr. 1-3
SSN1-40	Beatrix Potter Gr. 2-4
SSN1-129	Beatrix Potter: Activity Biography Gr. 2-4
SSB1-47	Beautiful Bugs Gr. 1
SSB1-21	Beavers Gr. 3-5
SSN1-257	Because of Winn-Dixie NS Gr. 4-6
SSR1-53	Beginning Manuscript Gr. Pk-2
SSR1-54	Beginning Cursive Gr. 2-4
SSR1-57	Beginning and Practice Manuscript Gr. PK-2
SSR1-58	Beginning and Practice Cursive Gr. 2-4
SSN1-33	Bedtime for Frances NS 1-3
SSN1-114	Best Christmas Pageant Ever NS Gr. 4-6
SSN1-32	Best Friends for Frances NS Gr. 1-3
SSB1-39	Best Friends Pets Gr. P-K
SSN1-185	BFG NS Gr. 4-6
SSJ1-61	Big Book of Canadian Celebrations Gr. 1-3
SSJ1-62	Big Book of Canadian Celebrations Gr. 4-6
SSN1-35	Birthday for Frances NS Gr. 1-3
SSN1-107	Borrowers NS Gr. 4-6
SSC1-16	Bouquet of Valentines Gr. 2
SSN1-29	Bread & Jam for Frances NS Gr. 1-3
SSN1-63	Bridge to Terabithia NS Gr. 4-6
SSY1-24	BTS Numeración Gr. 1-3
SSY1-25	BTS Adición Gr. 1-3
SSY1-26	BTS Sustracción Gr. 1-3
SSY1-27	BTS Fonética Gr. 1-3
SSY1-28	BTS Leer para Entender Gr. 1-3
SSY1-29	BTS Uso de las Mayúsculas y Reglas de Puntuación Gr. 1-3
SSY1-30	BTS Composición de Oraciones Gr. 1-3
SSY1-31	BTS Composici13n de Historias Gr. 1-3
SSN1-256	Bud, Not Buddy NS Gr. 4-6
SSB1-31	Bugs, Bugs & More Bugs Gr. 2-3
SSR1-07	Building Word Families L.V. Gr. 1-2
SSR1-05	Building Word Families S.V. Gr. 1-2
SSN1-204	Bunnicula NS Gr. 4-6
SSB1-80	Butterflies & Caterpillars Gr. 1-2
SSN1-164	Call It Courage NS Gr. 7-8
SSN1-67	Call of the Wild NS Gr. 7-8
SSJ1-41	Canada & It's Trading Partners 6-8
SSPC-28	Canada B/W Pictures
SSN1-173	Canada Geese Quilt NS Gr. 4-6
SSJ1-01	Canada Gr. 1
SSJ1-33	Canada's Capital Cities Gr. 4-6
SSJ1-43	Canada's Confederation Gr. 7-8
SSF1-04	Canada's First Nations Gr. 7-8
SSJ1-51	Canada's Landmarks Gr. 1-3
SSJ1-48	Canada's Landmarks Gr. 4-6
SSJ1-60	Canada's Links to the World Gr. 5-8
SSJ1-42	Canada's Traditions & Celeb. Gr. 1-3
SSB1-45	Canadian Animals Gr. 1-2
SSJ1-37	Canadian Arctic Inuit Gr. 2-3
SSJ1-53	Canadian Black History Gr. 4-8
SSJ1-57	Canadian Comprehension Gr. 1-2
SSJ1-58	Canadian Comprehension Gr. 3-4
SSJ1-59	Canadian Comprehension Gr. 5-6
SSJ1-46	Canadian Industries Gr. 4-6
SSK1-12	Canadian Problem Solving Gr. 4-6
SSJ1-38	Canadian Provinces & Terr. Gr. 4-6
SSY1-07	Capitalization & Punctuation Gr. 1-3
SSN1-198	Captain Courageous NS Gr. 7-8
SSK1-11	Cars Problem Solving Gr. 3-4
SSN1-154	Castle in the Attic NS Gr. 4-6
SSF1-31	Castles & Kings Gr. 4-6
SSN1-144	Cat Ate My Gymsuit NS Gr. 4-6
SSPC-38	Cats B/W Pictures
SSB1-50	Cats – Domestic & Wild Gr. 4-6
SSN1-34	Cats in Literature Gr. 3-6
SSN1-212	Cay NS Gr. 7-8
SSM1-09	Celebrate Autumn Gr. 4-6
SSC1-39	Celebrate Christmas Gr. 4-6
SSC1-31	Celebrate Easter Gr. 4-6
SSC1-23	Celebrate Shamrock Day Gr. 2
SSM1-11	Celebrate Spring Gr. 4-6
SSC1-13	Celebrate Thanksgiving R. 3-4
SSM1-06	Celebrate Winter Gr. 4-6
SSB1-107	Cells, Tissues & Organs Gr. 7-8
SSB1-101	Characteristics of Flight Gr. 4-6
SSN1-66	Charlie & Chocolate Factory NS Gr. 4-6
SSN1-23	Charlotte's Web NS Gr. 4-6
SSB1-37	Chicks N'Ducks Gr. 2-4
SSA1-09	China Today Gr. 5-8
SSN1-70	Chocolate Fever NS Gr. 4-6
SSN1-241	Chocolate Touch NS Gr. 4-6
SSC1-38	Christmas Around the World Gr. 4-6
SSPC-42	Christmas B/W Pictures
SST1-08A	Christmas Gr. JK/SK
SST1-08B	Christmas Gr. 1
SST1-08C	Christmas Gr. 2-3
SSC1-04	Christmas Magic Gr. 1
SSC1-03	Christmas Tales Gr. 2-3
SSG1-06	Cinematography Gr. 5-8
SSPC-13	Circus B/W Pictures
SSF1-03	Circus Magic Gr. 3-4
SSJ1-52	Citizenship/Immigration Gr. 4-8
SSN1-104	Classical Poetry Gr. 7-12
SSN1-227	Color Gr. 1-3
SSN1-203	Colour Gr. 1-3
SSN1-135	Come Back Amelia Bedelia NS 1-3
SSH1-11	Community Helpers Gr. 1-3
SSK1-02	Concept Cards & Activities Gr. P-1
SSN1-183	Copper Sunrise NS Gr. 7-8
SSN1-86	Corduroy & Pocket Corduroy NS 1-3
SSN1-124	Could Dracula Live in Wood NS 4-6
SSN1-148	Cowboy's Don't Cry NS Gr. 7-8
SSR1-01	Creativity with Food Gr. 4-8
SSB1-34	Creatures of the Sea Gr. 2-4
SSN1-208	Curse of the Viking Grave NS 7-8
SSN1-134	Danny Champion of World NS 4-6
SSN1-98	Danny's Run NS Gr. 7-8
SSK1-21	Data Management Gr. 4-6
SSB1-53	Dealing with Dinosaurs Gr. 4-6
SSN1-178	Dear Mr. Henshaw NS Gr. 4-6
SSB1-22	Deer Gr. 3-5
SSPC-20	Desert B/W Pictures
SSJ1-40	Development of Western Canada 7-8
SSA1-16	Development of Manufacturing 7-9
SSN1-105	Dicken's Christmas NS Gr. 7-8
SSN1-62	Different Dragons NS Gr. 4-6
SSPC-21	Dinosaurs B/W Pictures
SSB1-16	Dinosaurs Gr. 1
SST1-02A	Dinosaurs Gr. JK/SK
SST1-02B	Dinosaurs Gr. 1
SST1-02 C	Dinosaurs Gr. 2-3
SSN1-175	Dinosaurs in Literature Gr. 1-3
SSJ1-26	Discover Nova Scotia Gr. 5-7
SSJ1-36	Discover Nunavut Territory Gr. 5-7
SSJ1-25	Discover Ontario Gr. 5-7
SSJ1-24	Discover PEI Gr. 5-7
SSJ1-22	Discover Québec Gr. 5-7
SSL1-01	Discovering the Library Gr. 2-3
SSB1-106	Diversity of Living Things Gr. 4-6
SSK1-27	Division Drills Gr. 4-6
SSB1-30	Dogs – Wild & Tame Gr. 4-6
SSPC-31	Dogs B/W Pictures
SSN1-196	Dog's Don't Tell Jokes NS Gr. 4-6
SSN1-182	Door in the Wall NS Gr. 4-6
SSB1-87	Down by the Sea Gr. 1-3
SSN1-189	Dr. Jeckyll & Mr. Hyde NS Gr. 4-6
SSG1-07	Dragon Trivia Gr. P-8
SSN1-102	Dragon's Egg NS Gr. 4-6
SSN1-16	Dragons in Literature Gr. 3-6
SSC1-06	Early Christmas Gr. 3-5
SSB1-109	Earth's Crust Gr. 6-8
SSC1-21	Easter Adventures Gr. 3-4
SSC1-17	Easter Delights Gr. P-K
SSC1-19	Easter Surprises Gr. 1
SSPC-12	Egypt B/W Pictures
SSN1-255	Egypt Game NS Gr. 4-6
SSF1-28	Egyptians Today & Yesterday Gr. 2-3
SSJ1-49	Elections in Canada Gr. 4-8
SSB1-108	Electricity Gr. 4-6
SSN1-02	Elves & the Shoemaker NS Gr. 1-3
SSH1-14	Emotions Gr. P-2
SSB1-85	Energy Gr. 4-6
SSN1-108	English Language Gr. 10-12
SSN1-156	Enjoying Eric Wilson Series Gr. 5-7
SSB1-64	Environment Gr. 4-6
SSR1-12	ESL Teaching Ideas Gr. K-8
SSN1-258	Esperanza Rising NS Gr. 4-6
SSR1-22	Exercises in Grammar Gr. 6
SSR1-23	Exercises in Grammar Gr. 7
SSR1-24	Exercises in Grammar Gr. 8
SSF1-20	Exploration Gr. 4-6
SSF1-15	Explorers & Mapmakers of Can. 7-8
SSJ1-54	Exploring Canada Gr. 1-3
SSJ1-56	Exploring Canada Gr. 1-6
SSJ1-55	Exploring Canada Gr. 4-6
SSH1-20	Exploring My School & Community 1
SSPC-39	Fables B/W Pictures
SSN1-15	Fables Gr. 4-6
SSN1-04	Fairy Tale Magic Gr. 3-5
SSPC-11	Fairy Tales B/W Pictures
SSN1-11	Fairy Tales Gr. 1-2
SSN1-199	Family Under the Bridge NS Gr. 4-6
SSPC-41	Famous Canadians B/W Pictures
SSJ1-12	Famous Canadians Gr. 4-8
SSN1-210	Fantastic Mr. Fox NS Gr. 4-6
SSB1-36	Fantastic Plants Gr. 4-6
SSPC-04	Farm Animals B/W Pictures
SSB1-15	Farm Animals Gr. 1-2
SST1-03A	Farm Gr. JK/SK
SST1-03B	Farm Gr. 1
SST1-03C	Farm Gr. 2-3
SSJ1-05	Farming Community Gr. 3-4
SSB1-44	Farmyard Friends Gr. P-K
SSJ1-45	Fathers of Confederation Gr. 4-8
SSB1-19	Feathered Friends Gr. 4-6
SST1-05A	February Gr. JK/SK
SST1-05B	February Gr. 1
SST1-05C	February Gr. 2-3
SSN1-03	Festival of Fairytales Gr. 3-5
SSC1-36	Festivals Around the World Gr. 2-3
SSN1-168	First 100 Sight Words Gr. 1
SSC1-32	First Days at School Gr. 1
SSJ1-06	Fishing Community Gr. 3-4
SSN1-170	Flowers for Algernon NS Gr. 7-8
SSN1-261	Flat Stanley NS Gr. 1-3
SSN1-128	Fly Away Home NS Gr. 4-6
SSD1-05	Food: Fact, Fun & Fiction Gr. 1-3
SSD1-06	Food: Nutrition & Invention Gr. 4-6
SSB1-118	Force and Motion Gr. 1-3
SSB1-119	Force and Motion Gr. 4-6
SSB1-25	Foxes Gr. 3-5
SSN1-263	Fractured Fairy Tales NS Gr. 1-3
SSN1-172	Freckle Juice NS Gr. 1-3
SSB1-43	Friendly Frogs Gr. 1
SSN1-260	Frindle NS Gr. 4-6
SSB1-89	Fruits & Seeds Gr. 4-6
SSN1-137	Fudge-a-Mania NS Gr. 4-6
SSB1-14	Fun on the Farm Gr. 3-4
SSR1-49	Fun with Phonics Gr. 1-3
SSPC-06	Garden Flowers B/W Pictures
SSK1-03	Geometric Shapes Gr. 2-5
SSC1-18	Get the Rabbit Habit Gr. 1-2
SSN1-209	Giver, The NS Gr. 7-8
SSN1-190	Go Jump in the Pool NS Gr. 4-6
SSG1-03	Goal Setting Gr. 6-8
SSG1-08	Gr. 3 Test – Parent Guide
SSG1-99	Gr. 3 Test – Teacher Guide
SSG1-09	Gr. 6 Language Test–Parent Guide
SSG1-97	Gr. 6 Language Test–Teacher Guide
SSG1-10	Gr. 6 Math Test – Parent Guide
SSG1-96	Gr. 6 Math Test – Teacher Guide
SSG1-98	Gr. 6 Math/Lang. Test–Teacher Guide
SSK1-14	Graph for all Seasons Gr. 1-3
SSN1-117	Great Brain NS Gr. 4-6
SSN1-90	Great Expectations NS Gr. 7-8
SSN1-169	Great Gilly Hopkins NS Gr. 4-6
SSN1-197	Great Science Fair Disaster NS Gr. 4-6
SSN1-138	Greek Mythology Gr. 7-8
SSN1-113	Green Gables Detectives NS 4-6
SSC1-26	Groundhog Celebration Gr. 2
SSC1-25	Groundhog Day Gr. 1
SSB1-113	Growth & Change in Animals Gr. 2-3
SSB1-114	Growth & Change in Plants Gr. 2-3
SSB1-48	Guinea Pigs & Friends Gr. 3-5
SSB1-104	Habitats Gr. 4-6
SSPC-18	Halloween B/W Pictures
SST1-04A	Halloween Gr. JK/SK
SST1-04B	Halloween Gr. 1
SST1-04C	Halloween Gr. 2-3
SSC1-10	Halloween Gr. 4-6
SSC1-08	Halloween Happiness Gr. 1
SSC1-29	Halloween Spirits Gr. P-K
SSY1-13	Handwriting Manuscript Gr 1-3
SSY1-14	Handwriting Cursive Gr. 1-3
SSC1-42	Happy Valentines Day Gr. 3
SSN1-205	Harper Moon NS Gr. 7-8
SSN1-123	Harriet the Spy NS Gr. 4-6
SSC1-11	Harvest Time Wonders Gr. 1
SSN1-136	Hatchet NS Gr. 7-8
SSC1-09	Haunting Halloween Gr. 2-3
SSN1-91	Hawk & Stretch NS Gr. 4-6
SSC1-30	Hearts & Flowers Gr. P-K
SSN1-22	Heidi NS Gr. 4-6
SSN1-120	Help I'm Trapped in My NS Gr. 4-6
SSN1-24	Henry & the Clubhouse NS Gr. 4-6
SSN1-184	Hobbit NS Gr. 7-8
SSN1-122	Hoboken Chicken Emerg. NS 4-6
SSN1-250	Holes NS Gr. 4-6
SSN1-116	How Can a Frozen Detective NS 4-6
SSN1-89	How Can I be a Detective if I NS 4-6
SSN1-96	How Come the Best Clues... NS 4-6

Page 1 B-07

Publication Listing

Code #	Title and Grade
SSN1-133	How To Eat Fried Worms NS Gr.4-6
SSR1-48	How To Give a Presentation Gr. 4-6
SSN1-125	How To Teach Writing Through 7-9
SSR1-10	How To Write a Composition 6-10
SSR1-09	How To Write a Paragraph 5-10
SSR1-08	How To Write an Essay Gr. 7-12
SSR1-03	How To Write Poetry & Stories 4-6
SSD1-07	Human Body Gr. 2-4
SSD1-02	Human Body Gr. 4-6
SSN1-25	I Want to Go Home NS Gr. 4-6
SSH1-06	I'm Important Gr. 2-3
SSH1-07	I'm Unique Gr. 4-6
SSF1-05	In Days of Yore Gr. 4-6
SSF1-06	In Pioneer Days Gr. 2-4
SSM1-10	In the Wintertime Gr. 2
SSB1-41	Incredible Dinosaurs Gr. P-1
SSN1-177	Incredible Journey NS Gr. 4-6
SSN1-100	Indian in the Cupboard NS Gr. 4-6
SSPC-05	Insects B/W Pictures
SSPC-10	Inuit B/W Pictures
SSJ1-10	Inuit Community Gr. 3-4
SSN1-85	Ira Sleeps Over NS Gr. 1-3
SSN1-93	Iron Man NS Gr. 4-6
SSN1-193	Island of the Blue Dolphins NS 4-6
SSB1-11	It's a Dogs World Gr. 2-3
SSM1-05	It's a Marshmallow World Gr. 3
SSK1-05	It's About Time Gr. 2-4
SSC1-41	It's Christmas Time Gr. 3
SSH1-04	It's Circus Time Gr. 1
SSC1-43	It's Groundhog Day Gr. 3
SSB1-75	It's Maple Syrup Time Gr. 2-4
SSC1-40	It's Trick or Treat Time Gr. 2
SSN1-65	James & The Giant Peach NS 4-6
SSN1-106	Jane Eyre NS Gr. 7-8
SSPC-25	Japan B/W Pictures
SSA1-06	Japan Gr. 5-8
SSN1-264	Journey to the Centre of the Earth NS Gr. 7-8
SSC1-05	Joy of Christmas Gr. 2
SSN1-161	Julie of the Wolves NS Gr. 7-8
SSB1-81	Jungles Gr. 2-3
SSE1-02	Junior Music for Fall Gr. 4-6
SSE1-05	Junior Music for Spring Gr. 4-6
SSE1-06	Junior Music for Winter Gr. 4-6
SSR1-62	Just for Boys - Reading Comprehension Gr. 3-6
SSR1-63	Just for Boys - Reading Comprehension Gr. 6-8
SSN1-151	Kate NS Gr. 4-6
SSN1-95	Kidnapped in the Yukon NS Gr. 4-6
SSN1-140	Kids at Bailey School Gr. 2-4
SSN1-176	King of the Wind NS Gr. 4-6
SSF1-29	Klondike Gold Rush Gr. 4-6
SSF1-33	Labour Movement In Canada Gr. 7-8
SSN1-152	Lamplighter NS Gr. 4-6
SSB1-98	Learning About Dinosaurs Gr. 3
SSN1-38	Learning About Giants Gr. 4-6
SSK1-22	Learning About Measurement Gr. 1-3
SSB1-46	Learning About Mice Gr. 3-5
SSK1-09	Learning About Money CDN Gr. 1-3
SSK1-19	Learning About Money USA Gr. 1-3
SSK1-23	Learning About Numbers Gr. 1-3
SSB1-69	Learning About Rocks & Soils Gr. 2-3
SSK1-08	Learning About Shapes Gr. 1-3
SSB1-100	Learning About Simple Machines 1-3
SSK1-04	Learning About the Calendar Gr. 2-3
SSK1-10	Learning About Time Gr. 1-3
SSH1-17	Learning About Transportation Gr. 1
SSB1-02	Leaves Gr. 2-3
SSN1-50	Legends Gr. 4-6
SSC1-27	Lest We Forget Gr. 4-6
SSJ1-13	Let's Look at Canada Gr. 4-6
SSJ1-16	Let's Visit Alberta Gr. 2-4
SSJ1-15	Let's Visit British Columbia Gr. 2-4
SSJ1-03	Let's Visit Canada Gr. 3
SSJ1-18	Let's Visit Manitoba Gr. 2-4
SSJ1-21	Let's Visit New Brunswick Gr. 2-4
SSJ1-27	Let's Visit NFLD & Labrador Gr. 2-4
SSJ1-30	Let's Visit North West Terr. Gr. 2-4
SSJ1-20	Let's Visit Nova Scotia Gr. 2-4
SSJ1-34	Let's Visit Nunavut Gr. 2-4
SSJ1-17	Let's Visit Ontario Gr. 2-4
SSQ1-08	Let's Visit Ottawa Big Book Pkg 1-3
SSJ1-19	Let's Visit PEI Gr. 2-4
SSJ1-31	Let's Visit Québec Gr. 2-4
SSJ1-14	Let's Visit Saskatchewan Gr. 2-4
SSJ1-28	Let's Visit Yukon Gr. 2-4
SSN1-130	Life & Adv. of Santa Claus NS 7-8
SSB1-10	Life in a Pond Gr. 3-4
SSF1-30	Life in the Middle Ages Gr. 7-8
SSB1-103	Light & Sound Gr. 4-6

Code #	Title and Grade
SSN1-219	Light in the Forest NS Gr. 7-8
SSN1-121	Light on Hogback Hill NS Gr. 4-6
SSN1-46	Lion, Witch & the Wardrobe NS 4-6
SSR1-51	Literature Response Forms Gr. 1-3
SSR1-52	Literature Response Forms Gr. 4-6
SSN1-28	Little House Big Woods NS 4-6
SSN1-233	Little House on the Prairie NS 4-6
SSN1-111	Little Women NS Gr. 7-8
SSN1-115	Live from the Fifth Grade NS 4-6
SSN1-141	Look Through My Window NS 4-6
SSN1-112	Look! Visual Discrimination Gr. P-1
SSN1-61	Lost & Found NS Gr. 4-6
SSN1-109	Lost in the Barrens NS Gr. 7-8
SSJ1-08	Lumbering Community Gr. 3-4
SSN1-167	Magic School Bus Gr. 1-3
SSN1-247	Magic Treehouse Gr. 1-3
SSB1-78	Magnets Gr. 3-5
SSD1-03	Making Sense of Our Senses K-1
SSN1-146	Mama's Going to Buy You a NS 4-6
SSB1-94	Mammals Gr. 1
SSB1-95	Mammals Gr. 2
SSB1-96	Mammals Gr. 3
SSB1-97	Mammals Gr. 5-6
SSN1-160	Maniac Magee NS Gr. 4-6
SSA1-19	Mapping Activities & Outlines! 4-8
SSA1-17	Mapping Skills Gr. 1-3
SSA1-07	Mapping Skills Gr. 4-6
SST1-10A	March Gr. JK/SK
SST1-10B	March Gr. 1
SST1-10C	March Gr. 2-3
SSB1-57	Marvellous Marsupials Gr. 4-6
SSK1-01	Math Signs & Symbols Gr. 1-3
SSB1-116	Matter & Materials Gr. 1-3
SSB1-117	Matter & Materials Gr. 4-6
SSH1-03	Me, I'm Special! Gr. P-1
SSK1-16	Measurement Gr. 4-8
SSC1-02	Medieval Christmas Gr. 4-6
SSPC-09	Medieval Life B/W Pictures
SSC1-07	Merry Christmas Gr. P-K
SSK1-15	Metric Measurement Gr. 4-8
SSN1-13	Mice in Literature Gr. 3-5
SSB1-70	Microscopy Gr. 4-6
SSN1-180	Midnight Fox NS Gr. 4-6
SSN1-243	Midwife's Apprentice NS Gr. 4-6
SSJ1-07	Mining Community Gr. 3-4
SSK1-17	Money Talks – Cdn Gr. 3-6
SSK1-18	Money Talks – USA Gr. 3-6
SSB1-56	Monkeys & Apes Gr. 4-6
SSN1-43	Monkeys in Literature Gr. 2-4
SSN1-54	Monster Mania Gr. 4-6
SSN1-97	Mouse & the Motorcycle NS 4-6
SSN1-94	Mr. Poppers Penguins NS Gr. 4-6
SSN1-201	Mrs. Frisby & Rats NS Gr. 4-6
SSR1-13	Multi-Level Spelling Program Gr. 3-6
SSR1-26	Multi-Level Spelling USA Gr. 3-6
SSK1-31	Addition & Subtraction Drills 1-3
SSK1-32	Multiplication & Division Drills 4-6
SSK1-30	Multiplication Drills Gr. 4-6
SSA1-14	My Country! The USA! Gr. 2-4
SSN1-186	My Side of the Mountain NS 7-8
SSN1-58	Mysteries, Monsters & Magic Gr. 6-8
SSN1-37	Mystery at Blackrock Island NS 7-8
SSN1-80	Mystery House NS 4-6
SSN1-157	Nate the Great & Sticky Case NS 1-3
SSF1-23	Native People of North America 4-6
SSF1-25	New France Part 1 Gr. 7-8
SSF1-27	New France Part 2 Gr. 7-8
SSA1-10	New Zealand Gr. 4-8
SSN1-51	Newspapers Gr. 5-8
SSN1-47	No Word for Goodbye NS Gr. 7-8
SSPC-03	North American Animals B/W Pictures
SSF1-22	North American Natives Gr. 2-4
SSN1-75	Novel Ideas Gr. 4-6
SST1-06A	November JK/SK
SST1-06B	November Gr. 1
SST1-06C	November Gr. 2-3
SSN1-244	Number the Stars NS Gr. 4-6
SSY1-03	Numeration Gr. 1-3
SSPC-14	Nursery Rhymes B/W Pictures
SSN1-12	Nursery Rhymes Gr. P-1
SSN1-59	On the Banks of Plum Creek NS 4-6
SSN1-220	One in Middle Green Kangaroo NS 1-3
SSN1-145	One to Grow On NS Gr. 4-6
SSB1-27	Opossums Gr. 3-5
SSJ1-23	Ottawa Gr. 7-9
SSJ1-39	Our Canadian Governments Gr. 5-8
SSF1-14	Our Global Heritage Gr. 4-6
SSH1-12	Our Neighbourhoods Gr. 4-6
SSB1-72	Our Trash Gr. 2-3
SSB1-51	Our Universe Gr. 5-8
SSB1-86	Outer Space Gr. 1-2
SSA1-18	Outline Maps of the World Gr. 1-8

Code #	Title and Grade
SSB1-67	Owls Gr. 4-6
SSN1-31	Owls in the Family NS Gr. 4-6
SSL1-02	Oxbridge Owl & The Library Gr. 4-6
SSB1-71	Pandas, Polar & Penguins Gr. 4-6
SSN1-52	Paperbag Princess NS Gr. 1-3
SSR1-11	Passion of Jesus: A Play Gr. 7-8
SSA1-12	Passport to Adventure Gr. 4-5
SSR1-06	Passport to Adventure Gr. 7-8
SSR1-04	Personal Spelling Dictionary Gr. 2-5
SSPC-29	Pets B/W Pictures
SSE1-03	Phantom of the Opera Gr. 7-9
SSN1-171	Phoebe Gilman Author Study Gr. 2-3
SSY1-06	Phonics Gr. 1-3
SSK1-33	Picture Math Book Gr. 1-3
SSN1-237	Pierre Berton Author Study Gr. 7-8
SSN1-179	Pigman NS Gr. 7-8
SSN1-48	Pigs in Literature Gr. 2-4
SSN1-99	Pinballs NS Gr. 4-6
SSN1-60	Pippi Longstocking NS Gr. 4-6
SSF1-12	Pirates Gr. 4-6
SSK1-13	Place Value Gr. 4-6
SSB1-77	Planets Gr. 3-6
SSR1-74	Poetry Prompts Gr. 1-3
SSR1-75	Poetry Prompts Gr. 4-6
SSB1-66	Popcorn Fun Gr. 2-3
SSB1-20	Porcupines Gr. 3-5
SSR1-55	Practice Manuscript Gr. Pk-2
SSR1-56	Practice Cursive Gr. 2-4
SSF1-24	Prehistoric Times Gr. 4-6
SSE1-01	Primary Music for Fall Gr. 1-3
SSE1-04	Primary Music for Spring Gr. 1-3
SSE1-07	Primary Music for Winter Gr. 1-3
SSJ1-47	Prime Ministers of Canada Gr. 4-8
SSN1-262	Prince Caspian NS Gr. 4-6
SSK1-20	Probability & Inheritance Gr. 7-10
SSN1-49	Question of Loyalty NS Gr. 7-8
SSN1-26	Rabbits in Literature Gr. 2-4
SSB1-17	Raccoons Gr. 3-5
SSN1-207	Radio Fifth Grade NS Gr. 4-6
SSB1-52	Rainbow of Colours Gr. 4-6
SSN1-144	Ramona Quimby Age 8 NS 4-6
SSJ1-09	Ranching Community Gr. 3-4
SSY1-08	Reading for Meaning Gr. 1-3
SSR1-76	Reading Logs Gr. K-1
SSR1-77	Reading Logs Gr. 2-3
SSN1-165	Reading Response Forms Gr. 1-3
SSN1-239	Reading Response Forms Gr. 4-6
SSN1-234	Reading with Arthur Gr. 1-3
SSN1-249	Reading with Canadian Authors 1-3
SSN1-200	Reading with Curious George Gr. 2-4
SSN1-230	Reading with Eric Carle Gr. 1-3
SSN1-251	Reading with Kenneth Oppel Gr. 4-6
SSN1-127	Reading with Mercer Mayer Gr. 1-2
SSN1-07	Reading with Motley Crew Gr. 2-3
SSN1-142	Reading with Robert Munsch 1-3
SSN1-06	Reading with the Super Sleuths 4-6
SSN1-08	Reading with the Ziggles Gr. 1
SST1-11A	Red Gr. JK/SK
SSN1-147	Refuge NS Gr. 7-8
SSC1-44	Remembrance Day Gr. 1-3
SSPC-23	Reptiles B/W Pictures
SSB1-42	Reptiles Gr. 4-6
SSN1-110	Return of the Indian NS Gr. 4-6
SSN1-225	River NS Gr. 7-8
SSE1-08	Robert Schuman, Composer Gr. 6-9
SSN1-83	Robot Alert NS Gr. 4-6
SSB1-65	Rocks & Minerals Gr. 4-6
SSN1-149	Romeo & Juliet NS Gr. 7-8
SSB1-88	Romping Reindeer Gr. K-3
SSN1-21	Rumplestiltskin NS Gr. 1-3
SSN1-153	Runaway Ralph NS Gr. 4-6
SSN1-103	Sadako & 1000 Paper Cranes NS 4-6
SSD1-04	Safety Gr. 2-4
SSN1-42	Sarah Plain & Tall NS Gr. 4-6
SSC1-34	School in September Gr. 4-6
SSPC-01	Sea Creatures B/W Pictures
SSB1-79	Sea Creatures Gr. 1-3
SSN1-64	Secret Garden NS Gr. 4-6
SSB1-90	Seeds & Weeds Gr. 2-3
SSY1-02	Sentence Writing Gr. 1-3
SST1-07A	September JK/SK
SST1-07B	September Gr. 1
SST1-07C	September Gr. 2-3
SSN1-30	Serendipity Series Gr. 3-5
SSC1-22	Shamrocks on Parade Gr. 1
SSC1-24	Shamrocks, Harps & Shillelaghs 3-4
SSR1-66	Shakespeare Shorts-Perf Arts Gr. 1-4
SSR1-67	Shakespeare Shorts-Perf Arts Gr. 4-6
SSR1-68	Shakespeare Shorts-Lang Arts Gr. 2-4
SSR1-69	Shakespeare Shorts-Lang Arts Gr. 4-6
SSB1-74	Sharks Gr. 4-6
SSN1-158	Shiloh NS Gr. 4-6

Code #	Title and Grade
SSN1-84	Sideways Stories Wayside NS 4-6
SSN1-181	Sight Words Activities Gr. 1
SSB1-99	Simple Machines Gr. 4-6
SSN1-19	Sixth Grade Secrets 4-6
SSG1-04	Skill Building with Slates Gr. K-8
SSN1-118	Skinny Bones NS Gr. 4-6
SSB1-24	Skunks Gr. 3-5
SSN1-191	Sky is Falling NS Gr. 4-6
SSB1-83	Slugs & Snails Gr. 1-3
SSB1-55	Snakes Gr. 4-6
SST1-12A	Snow Gr. JK/SK
SST1-12B	Snow Gr. 1
SST1-12C	Snow Gr. 2-3
SSB1-76	Solar System Gr. 4-6
SSPC-44	South America B/W Pictures
SSA1-11	South America Gr. 4-6
SSB1-05	Space Gr. 2-3
SSR1-34	Spelling Blacklines Gr. 1
SSR1-35	Spelling Blacklines Gr. 2
SSR1-36	Spelling Blacklines Gr. 3
SSR1-37	Spelling Blacklines Gr. 4
SSR1-14	Spelling Gr. 1
SSR1-15	Spelling Gr. 2
SSR1-16	Spelling Gr. 3
SSR1-17	Spelling Gr. 4
SSR1-18	Spelling Gr. 5
SSR1-19	Spelling Gr. 6
SSR1-27	Spelling Worksavers #1 Gr. 3-5
SSM1-02	Spring Celebration Gr. 2-3
SST1-01A	Spring Gr. JK/SK
SST1-01B	Spring Gr. 1
SST1-01C	Spring Gr. 2-3
SSM1-01	Spring in the Garden Gr. 1-2
SSB1-26	Squirrels Gr. 3-5
SSB1-112	Stable Structures & Mechanisms 3
SSG1-05	Steps in the Research Process 5-8
SSG1-02	Stock Market Gr. 7-8
SSN1-139	Stone Fox NS Gr. 4-6
SSN1-214	Stone Orchard NS Gr. 7-8
SSN1-01	Story Book Land of Witches Gr. 2-3
SSR1-64	Story Starters Gr. 1-3
SSR1-65	Story Starters Gr. 4-6
SSR1-73	Story Starters Gr. 1-6
SSY1-09	Story Writing Gr. 1-3
SSB1-111	Structures, Mechanisms & Motion 2
SSN1-211	Stuart Little NS Gr. 4-6
SSK1-29	Subtraction Drills Gr. 1-3
SSY1-05	Subtraction Gr. 1-3
SSY1-11	Successful Language Pract. Gr. 1-3
SSY1-12	Successful Math Practice Gr. 1-3
SSW1-09	Summer Learning Gr. K-1
SSW1-10	Summer Learning Gr. 1-2
SSW1-11	Summer Learning Gr. 2-3
SSW1-12	Summer Learning Gr. 3-4
SSW1-13	Summer Learning Gr. 4-5
SSW1-14	Summer Learning Gr. 5-6
SSN1-159	Summer of the Swans NS Gr. 4-6
SSZ1-02	Summer Olympics Gr. 4-6
SSM1-07	Super Summer Gr. 1-2
SSN1-18	Superfudge NS Gr. 4-6
SSA1-08	Switzerland Gr. 4-6
SSN1-20	T.V. Kid NS. Gr. 4-6
SSA1-15	Take a Trip to Australia Gr. 2-3
SSB1-102	Taking Off With Flight Gr. 1-3
SSK1-34	Teaching Math with Everyday Munipulatives Gr. 4-6
SSN1-259	The Tale of Despereaux NS Gr. 4-6
SSN1-55	Tales of the Fourth Grade NS 4-6
SSN1-188	Taste of Blackberries NS Gr. 4-6
SSK1-07	Teaching Math Through Sports 6-9
SST1-09A	Thanksgiving JK/SK
SST1-09C	Thanksgiving Gr. 2-3
SSN1-77	There's a Boy in the Girls... NS 4-6
SSN1-143	This Can't Be Happening NS 4-6
SSN1-05	Three Billy Goats Gruff NS Gr. 1-3
SSN1-72	Ticket to Curlew NS Gr. 4-6
SSN1-82	Timothy of the Cay NS Gr. 7-8
SSF1-32	Titanic Gr. 4-6
SSN1-222	To Kill a Mockingbird NS Gr. 7-8
SSN1-195	Toilet Paper Tigers NS Gr. 4-6
SSJ1-35	Toronto Gr. 4-8
SSH1-02	Toy Shelf Gr. P-K
SSPC-24	Toys B/W Pictures
SSN1-163	Traditional Poetry Gr. 7-10
SSH1-13	Transportation Gr. 4-6
SSW1-01	Transportation Snip Art
SSB1-03	Trees Gr. 2-3
SSA1-01	Tropical Rainforest Gr. 4-6
SSN1-56	Trumpet of the Swan NS Gr. 4-6
SSN1-81	Tuck Everlasting NS Gr. 4-6
SSN1-126	Turtles in Literature Gr. 1-3
SSN1-45	Underground to Canada NS 4-6

Publication Listing

Code #	Title and Grade
SSN1-27	Unicorns in Literature Gr. 3-5
SSJ1-44	Upper & Lower Canada Gr. 7-8
SSN1-192	Using Novels Canadian North Gr. 7-8
SSC1-14	Valentines Day Gr. 5-8
SSPC-45	Vegetables B/W Pictures
SSY1-01	Very Hungry Caterpillar NS 30/Pkg Gr. 1-3
SSF1-13	Victorian Era Gr. 7-8
SSC1-35	Victorian Christmas Gr. 5-8
SSF1-17	Viking Age Gr. 4-6
SSN1-206	War with Grandpa SN Gr. 4-6
SSB1-91	Water Gr. 2-4
SSN1-166	Watership Down NS Gr. 7-8
SSH1-16	Ways We Travel Gr. P-K
SSN1-101	Wayside Sch. Little Stranger NS Gr. 4-6
SSN1-76	Wayside Sch. is Falling Down NS 4-6
SSB1-60	Weather Gr. 4-6
SSN1-17	Wee Folk in Literature Gr. 3-5
SSPC-08	Weeds B/W Pictures
SSQ1-04	Welcome Back – Big Book Pkg 1-3
SSB1-73	Whale Preservation Gr. 5-8
SSH1-08	What is a Community? Gr. 2-4
SSH1-01	What is a Family? Gr. 2-3
SSH1-09	What is a School? Gr. 1-2
SSJ1-32	What is Canada? Gr. P-K
SSN1-79	What is RAD? Read & Discover 2-4
SSB1-62	What is the Weather Today? Gr. 2-4
SSN1-194	What's a Daring Detective NS 4-6
SSH1-10	What's My Number Gr. P-K
SSR1-02	What's the Scoop on Words Gr. 4-6
SSN1-73	Where the Red Fern Grows NS Gr. 7-8
SSN1-87	Where the Wild Things Are NS Gr. 1-3
SSN1-187	Whipping Boy NS Gr. 4-6
SSN1-226	Who is Frances Rain? NS Gr. 4-6
SSN1-74	Who's Got Gertie & How...? NS Gr. 4-6
SSN1-131	Why did the Underwear ... NS 4-6
SSC1-28	Why Wear a Poppy? Gr. 2-3
SSJ1-11	Wild Animals of Canada Gr. 2-3
SSPC-07	Wild Flowers B/W Pictures
SSB1-18	Winter Birds Gr. 2-3
SSZ1-03	Winter Olympics Gr. 4-6
SSM1-04	Winter Wonderland Gr. 1
SSC1-01	Witches Gr. 3-4
SSN1-213	Wolf Island NS Gr. 1-3
SSE1-09	Wolfgang Amadeus Mozart 6-9
SSB1-23	Wolves Gr. 3-5
SSC1-20	Wonders of Easter Gr. 2
SSY1-15	Word Families Gr. 1-3
SSR1-59	Word Families 2,3 Letter Words Gr. 1-3
SSR1-60	Word Families 3, 4 Letter Words Gr. 1-3
SSR1-61	Word Families 2, 3, 4 Letter Words Big Book Gr. 1-3
SSB1-35	World of Horses Gr. 4-6
SSB1-13	World of Pets Gr. 2-3
SSF1-26	World War II Gr. 7-8
SSN1-221	Wrinkle in Time NS Gr. 7-8
SSPC-02	Zoo Animals B/W Pictures
SSB1-08	Zoo Animals Gr. 1-2
SSB1-09	Zoo Celebration Gr. 3-4